Rambling for Pleasure

The Secrets
OF
Countryside Access

Dave Ramm

Contents

The Ramblers

Published by
The East Berkshire Ramblers'
Association Group

ISBN 1-874258-20-1

Copyright © Dave Ramm 2006
First published in the UK 2006

Acknowledgements
Written by: Dave Ramm
Design by: David Rose
Maps by: Paul Hopgood
Printed by: Gutenberg Press Ltd, Malta

All photographs are by the author
unless otherwise stated.
Pages 4 and 6 courtesy of:
*The Museum of English Rural Life,
The University of Reading.*

Front cover:
View from The Saddle Knob in Surrey.
Grid ref. TQ243521.
Photos of Nick Crane courtesy of Tern TV

OS Map extracts reproduced from
Exlporer 1:25 000 by permission of
Ordnance Survey on behalf of The
Controller of Her Majesty's Stationery
Office. © Crown copyright 2006.
All rights reserved.
Licence number 100020045

Foreword by Nick Crane

My first walking expedition was a three-day hike through the Peak District with my mother. I was in my early teens. We slept at youth hostels and our route included Dovedale, which I remember as a wildly exotic gorge. With a dog-eared one-inch-to-the-mile map, I began exploring the countryside, an activity which eventually led to a 10,000-kilometre hike across Europe's mountain ranges.

All those early walks with Ordnance Survey maps paid off, for I was frequently trying to find my way across inadedequately surveyed peaks and passes, sometimes in storms and cloud. For months in the Carpathians, I had to rely upon my compass and one-hundred-year-old military road maps, an experience which reminded me that we in Britain are the luckiest hikers on the planet. Not only are Ordnance Survey maps the best in the world for walking, but we have an unparalleled network of public paths. Anybody who has stepped off tarmac onto a field-path or bridleway will know the surge of pleasure and expectation which accompanies the transition into that quieter, calmer world. These byways are one of these country's most precious assets, handed down through time and kept open by the passage of feet. Each generation takes custody of them, and hands them on to the next.

In this era of climatic change, we must look to our local landscapes if we are to grasp the fragility and transience of our natural habitat. There is no better place to appreciate the wonder and complexity of our magical biosphere, than from public footpath, common and open down. And this book will show you the way.

Nick Crane – TVs Mapman

The way we were. Arbrook Common, Surrey c1905

'The greatest joy is that they go somewhere, these footpaths of ours. They are not just sterile 'hiking trails' leading back round to the car park. They are ways of travelling. They link us to our pedestrian ancestors. They are precious'

Libby Purves, Journalist, Broadcaster and Author, Saga Jan. 2004

Introduction
A simple pleasure

The English countryside is at the heart of our national identity. Country folk, however, who are dependent upon the town for many of the products and facilities it offers, can sometimes be rather possessive of their own world and reluctant to accept outsiders on *their* patch – a world that many born in the town do not understand and can occasionally find hostile and intimidating.

A recent Countryside Commission (now Agency) survey showed that only 12% of the population felt they had enough information about the countryside. Hopefully, we can redress this situation somewhat in these few pages by sharing the answers to questions that I have asked myself, and that others have asked me, over the past 30 years about rambling in the countryside for pleasure.

Knowledge is power, they tell us, but I am not advocating that we all go strutting around demanding this and demanding that. Most of what we need is there already, on the statute books. All we need is for everyone to be better informed. Then walkers can be confident and, where necessary, a bit more assertive – in a polite and friendly way, of course.

Even though country walking is recognised as one of the nation's most favoured and healthy activities, there does seem to be a lack of motivation on the part of government and officials to address the issues. Local Authorities are responsible for maintaining all the highways, not just the metalled ones we drive along every day. Is it something to do with much of the countryside being literally *on the side* and therefore hidden from view? If only some of the problems were a little more *in their face*, additional resources might be forthcoming.

This book will hopefully prompt more walkers to see more of our country, to find more of our paths and if necessary bring them to light when they are under threat or simply need to be made a little more suitable for ordinary folk and families, not just 'committed' ramblers.

I look forward to the day when farmers and landowners are happy to see lots of people using all the paths and walkers think they would like to pass the time of day with them, and the feel-good factor abounds.

Quite often it already does.

Those were the days, when the sun always shone. (Near Cookham in Berkshire. c1905)

A Fortunate Inheritance

Many of the paths that we can use today have an ancient history; created from medieval times as routes linking villages, hamlets and farms. Local people used them to get to church, mill or market or to other homesteads. The routes that people chose came naturally to them. Whenever possible they took the shortest route, aiming to cross a stream at the most convenient point, yet avoiding a steep climb or a road that became impassable in winter. The modern term **desire path** succinctly illustrates just how they came about. Fortunately, the antiquity of such paths can often still be seen and experienced.

However, the notion that what used to be called field paths might also be used for pleasure is not new. The novels of Jane Austen and Thomas Hardy abound in references to walks taken for recreational purposes on public paths. During the industrial revolution, people of all classes turned to the countryside for relaxation and enjoyment. Children played on them and Sunday walks or an evening stroll were an integral part of English rural life during the 19th century. Where you could walk was simply local knowledge, handed down from one generation to the next.

In the immediate post-war years, the government decided to address the muddle of case law that had largely governed the use of paths. The great majority of the rights that we exercise today came about because of what is now referred to as **deemed dedication**; the law presumes that at some time in the past a landowner effectively dedicated a way by not making any objection

'Nobody can't stop'ee. – It's a footpath, right enough.'

Edward Thomas, Poet and nature writer (1878-1917)

The Church Path. Surely the most distinctive manifestation of a man–made 'desire line'.

A modern desire-path; a direct route created naturally in an urban setting.

to the use of it by the public. Providing there was no evidence to the contrary, this right was deemed to have been dedicated at the end of a 20-year period and in 1949 the **National Parks and Access to the Countryside Act** required County Councils, as the surveying authority, to identify these ways by reference to parish records and to officially record them.

Although it is now apparent that many forgotten or little used paths were overlooked, if a way is shown on the **Definitive Map**, it is legal, conclusive evidence that the public have a right of passage along it. All county councils and unitary authorities are required to hold copies, to keep them up to date and to display them at their offices. On these relatively large-scale maps, every path within a parish is given a number. Occasionally, where a path itself forms the boundary between parishes, it may be numbered independently in each of them.

Accompanying this map is the **Definitive Statement**. This lists every path in each parish, states what type of way it is and where it starts and finishes. Some may also give a width, note any limitations such as stiles, gates or bridges, and perhaps a brief route description. Together with the map, this is the basis for many of the rights that we exercise in our countryside today.

Some of the original parish records held by Oxfordshire County Council describing routes for inclusion on the definitive map.

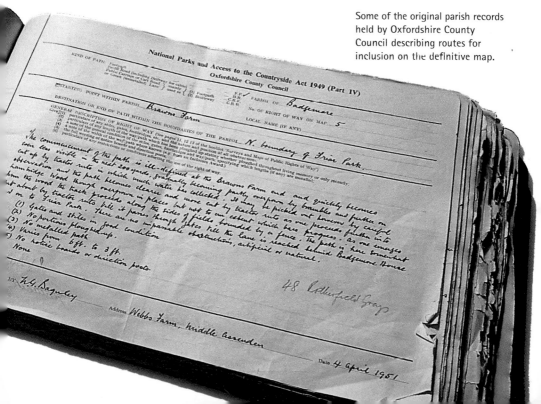

Key to the Countryside
A study of the Explorer Map

The most important tool for exploring the countryside on your own for the first time is a good map and the most detailed and comprehensive source of such information is the Ordnance Survey **Explorer Map**. We shall concentrate exclusively on this series because they are ideal for walkers. Other maps are generally at a smaller scale with less detail, which can make way-finding more difficult.

This set of 470 maps now covers the whole country, excluding the Isle of Man, where the Manx Government does the honours. Start by purchasing the sheet that covers the area where you live; look for the orange cover. This is probably the most important countryside to you because it is convenient and easily accessible. Most bookshops, information centres, larger newsagents, outdoor leisure shops and some garages stock local OS maps. Some of the two-sided sheets are especially good value.

By far the easiest and most enjoyable way to practise reading this map will be to take a short walk in the countryside with it. In this relaxed setting, without the fear of traffic queueing up behind, you will be able to wander along examining the map closely and comparing it to the world around you before deciding on the next path that you want to take. However, like any product that we are not familiar with, first we need to take some time to understand what the map tells us and how it works.

When you first open out the map, it can all look very confusing. Most conspicuous may be the built-up areas, followed by the motorways and other main roads. Our paths lie hidden away between all these busy modern arteries. At this **scale** (1:25 000), everything on the ground is actually twenty-five thousand times bigger than on the map.

With a map scale written as 1: 25 000, the unit *1* is the length on the map and the figure *25,000* is the comparable distance on the ground. So, for example, one inch on the map equates with 25,000 inches (about two-fifths of a mile) on the ground. Likewise, one millimetre on the map is equal to 25,000 millimetres (25 metres) on the ground. A footpath measuring four centimetres on the map will involve a walk of one kilometre (4 cm x 25,000 = 100,000 cm). Judging these comparative distances is made easier by always using the same scale of map.

The map we are using is called a **topographic map**. That is to say, unlike a road atlas, for example, its primary aim is to show in great detail all the natural and man-made features (the topography) that we can see around us. It will include, for instance, every wood, building, road, and path (whether or not the public can use it) that was evident on the ground at the time of the survey.

Added to this topographical detail is information from other sources, in particular the administrative boundaries, the access land and (from the Definitive Map) the position of all the **public rights of way**. These various green dashes, showing the ground over which the public has a right to pass, are probably the single most important element of the map for us. Usually, the definitive path will be coincident with a path that actually exists on the ground, but for various reasons this may not always be so. (See Chapter 10, development, and

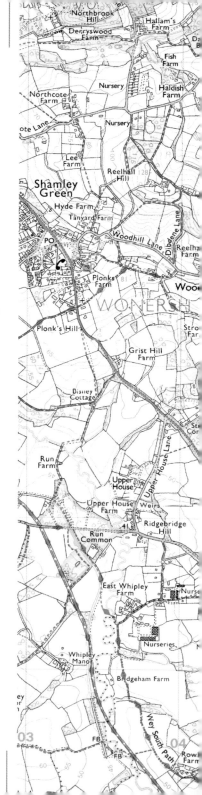

All land is owned by someone.

the map anomalies illustrated on page 30.) Any route observed on the ground at the time of the survey will be shown in black with the 'legal' routes added in green.

Before we detail the options available to us, it is important to realise that all the land shown on our map, is owned by someone. Nearly all of it is **private land**. But it is equally important to appreciate that the public do have various rights of way over some of it – literally, ways which are open *as of right* to all members of the public. Every different type of way, from the meandering footpath to the roaring motorway, forms part of the Queen's Highway and has the same protection in law. What varies is the mode of travelling permitted on the different types of way. (Strictly, only the motorway is not available to walkers.) As we shall see, this in turn largely dictates the nature of the way itself.

The most humble way is the public **footpath**. It is also often the most intimate and sometimes the hardest to find. Walkers share it only with other walkers – and wildlife if you're lucky. Look for the fine, green dashes on the map. In 1861 it was held to be legal to take a pushchair as a natural accompaniment, but the surface may not always be suitable. To avoid stiles and gates being a problem, those with young children may like to consider bridleways, byways or the towpath as a better option. Another alternative is to examine the map closely and identify those public footpaths which are actually along tracks rather than across fields, for example. Incidentally a bicycle is *not* considered a natural accompaniment for a walker – even if you are pushing it.

Somewhat more prominent on our map is the **bridleway**, which walkers share with horse-riders and, since 1968, with cyclists. However, cyclists should give way to walkers and there is no requirement for the surface, which may be temporally disturbed at times during the farming year, to be made especially suitable for them. Look for the longer and more significant green dashes.

You may still find the classification **'Road Used as Public Path'** (RUPP) on your map. However, as a result of the uncertainty regarding vehicular rights over them, a new category of right of way was created by the CRoW Act 2000. Over the coming years, most of these will probably be reclassified as **Restricted Byways**. They may be used by horse-drawn vehicles but not by mechanically propelled vehicles, unless evidence of full vehicular rights can be proved. You will notice that they appear similar to the bridleway symbol on the map but with a small bar on alternate sides of the broken green line. As an interim measure, you may find some counties have signed these thoroughfares simply 'Right of Way'.

Driving, but not as we know it; gently and unobtrusively along restricted byways. Bruce Blundell with Emma near Ropley, Hampshire.
Photo: ©Alec Fry

Motorised users on byways open to all traffic, must show consideration for others.

On some routes, walkers may have to share the way with motorised vehicles. These are classified as **Byway Open to All Traffic** (BOAT) and are shown with the bridleway symbol but with a bar across the broken green line. These routes originally became established as vehicular highways used by horses and carts and where the surface has not been improved, it can easily be damaged by motor bikes and heavy, four-wheel-drive vehicles.

A few **Permitted Paths** (or 'permissive' paths) and bridleways may also be available to us. Those notified to the Ordnance Survey are shown on the Explorer map; look for the orange/brown dashes. Paths should only be provided by the landowner as an additional route and not as an alternative to a legitimate path. Some counties and unitary authorities hold a list of those routes that the landowner has formally agreed to provide. However, they have no legal status and the duty of care to users lies entirely with the landowner. Permission to use them can be withdrawn at any time. Other non-definitive paths may be closed for one day each year to prevent a claim for right of way status.

Some **towpaths** alongside canals such as the Kennet & Avon are dedicated as rights of way, but others such as Basingstoke Canal are not. The British Waterways Board generally allows the public to use all of them. However, you may have to look closely at the OS map to see either the annotation 'Towing Path' or the fence line to an adjacent field set back from the bank, to distinguish which side of the canal any non-definitive path follows. Towing paths alongside navigable rivers often became truncated when ferry operations ceased. Recently, pressure to avoid road walking has focused attention on replacing some of these locations with footbridges, or very occasionally by reintroducing a limited ferry service where demand exists.

Walk or cycle the Down Link bridleway – the last train through this station was more than 40 years ago!

Following the Beeching Report of 1963, some local authorities were quicker than others to appreciate the recreational value of **redundant branch lines**. Nearly all the 33 miles of track-bed from south of Guildford to the South Downs is now on the definitive map as the Downs Link bridleway. But a stretch of eight miles of dismantled railway available to us in Hampshire, is only apparent because it is highlighted as a recreational route and cycleway, part of the Test Way. Other short sections have been designated as public footpaths and some de facto access exists where routes are not built over or obstructed by fences.

The acorn symbol indicates a National Trail.

The Thames Path and The Ridgeway are two of this region's most well-known **National Trails**. Maintenance and promotion of such officially designated routes is grant-aided by the Countryside Agency with help from local authorities. In England and Wales, look out for the acorn symbol displayed at intervals along the way itself.

Clear and durable national trail signs made from recycled plastic.

Cyclists should note that most of the Thames Path is a designated footpath!

This green lane, shown on the map with green dots, may not be signed in any way as it is officially just an ordinary road, like any other.

Together with selected **recreational paths** that have been devised by other organisations and individuals, they are shown on the Explorer map using a green diamond notation. These longer-distance routes are usually coincident with rights of way. Occasionally, where the diamond symbol stands alone, it can identify other paths that we may use, but which are not on the definitive map, for example, a way across Ascot Heath and the race-course, used by our Three Castles Path en route from Windsor to Winchester. (Incidentally, this is closed on one day of the year in November to avoid a claim for right of way status).

Signs and logos indicating and promoting other more parochial or circular routes (CR) are now very common, although it only takes one to go missing for walkers, tempted to rely on them, to be lost.

Inevitably, as you study the Explorer Map, you will see some fine, black, double lines. As they have no colour infill, they are sometimes referred to as **white roads**. On the ground, they are often unsurfaced tracks between banks or hedges, perhaps of some antiquity, which can give rise to the alternative descriptive term **green lane**. It is all rather a grey area! You can only be certain if they have public rights when the map shows them superimposed with green dots, in which case they will appear on the Highway Authority list of streets that are publicly maintainable. Walkers can also sometimes profit from short lengths of old road where, we hope, pedestrian rights were maintained when the new road was constructed. Look closely for this opportunity to avoid busy roads.

In 2000 Sustrans was awarded more than 42 million

pounds towards creating a **National Cycle Network** across the country. You will see some of these routes numbered in red on the map and indicated by orange spots where they coincide with public footpaths. Often, Sustrans have simply gone ahead and made permissive agreements with landowners to allow cycle access rather than use the Cycle Tracks Act 1984 or create purpose-built routes. Such agreements do not change the legal status of a footpath, but, as a result, walkers are now obliged to share these particular footpaths with cyclists.

Here Sustrans have made an agreement with the landowner for cyclists to use this public footpath across his land.

All that remains is to examine the key that appears in the margin of every OS map where all the **symbols** chosen to represent both the man-made and natural features that you may come across are explained. Where map detail is congested, look out for the blue arrow or 'lead-line' sometimes needed to precisely locate tourist information such as car parks. And if it is refreshments that you need, remember that the Post Office, if it still exists, (PO on our map) is also probably the village shop.

Shown in grey are the various names and delineations representing county, civil parish (CP) and other **administrative boundaries**. Evidence of these can sometimes be found in the form of banks, ditches and markers on the ground, but walkers most frequently use these details to identify the parish if there is a problem to be reported.

A landowner can allow other users (in this case horse riders) onto his land, providing they do not damage the way or interfere with public rights.

Spend an evening studying the contents of this marginal information panel, looking for examples of each symbol and notation on the map itself, before setting off.

To supplement a collection of Explorer maps, country-lovers may like to consider a few **Landranger** sheets (also from the OS). They include a considerable amount of detail including public rights of way, but we cannot recommend that walkers use them to follow paths, primarily because they do not show the field boundaries and are only half the scale of our Explorer map series. However, their relatively large coverage area does make them useful for planning countryside visits.

By contrast, the small **local footpath maps**, such as those produced by the Chiltern Society and our own Ramblers' Association Group (both drawn at the same scale as Explorer maps), cover quite a small area, but have been designed specifically for walkers as they show the definitive path numbers and often include extra ways that have been locally agreed. They are also likely to be revised more frequently to include the latest changes in the path network. Because the paths are shown so prominently, they can be helpful in devising a walk and for reporting problems by quoting the parish name and path number.

None of these maps can replace or reproduce the amount of important detail that walkers acquire with the OS Explorer map series. Bill Bryson, one of the world's great travel writers, considers them 'second to none'.

Beech trees offer a good surface to indicate the path–numbers shown on Chiltern Society footpath maps. (Pishill 8 – part of the Chiltern Way)
Map: ©Chiltern Society

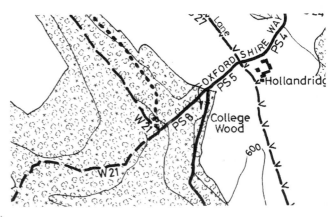

Getting into Gear
Preparation and clothing

We all spend so much time these days driving, or indoors with the central-heating on, that it is easy to underestimate what effect the elements can have on us out in the countryside. But, as any seasoned rambler will tell you, there is no such thing as bad weather, only inappropriate clothing. As we have always reminded readers of our guidebooks, you will need to be suitably clad.

Nobody wants to spend most of their time looking down, trying to avoid wet or muddy conditions under foot; it only takes one really bad section to cause some walkers to retrace their steps. So, some stout and comfortable **footwear** designed for the job (plus a pair of good quality walking socks) has to be a wise investment. It could save a twisted ankle too, on uneven ground. Go to one of the outdoor shops that employ trained staff who can give advice and help you choose from the dozens of products available.

The next most important items are some **waterproof garments**. There are dozens of specialist companies with a baffling array of new products on the market incorporating the latest materials and technology. Somehow, you will need to balance cost with effectiveness, weight and versatility.

Bear in mind that it is possible to get extremely wet in the countryside even though it is not actually raining. Long grass or a path through a crop that has not been kept clear to the required width can drench you up to the knees, even though it might have stopped raining

'Thrice blessed is our sunshine after rain'
George Meredith, Hampshire novelist, (1828-1909)

High summer: try and keep in the shade, wear a hat and take plenty to drink.

Autumn: remember to take your camera.

before you set off. A pair of gaiters may suffice but you could need a pair of over-trousers in lush summer growth.

It depends on how fashionable you want to be, but in most other respects it is possible to manage without further investment, providing you already have a choice of year-round garments that can be worn in layers to keep you warm and the wind at bay. However, wearing jeans is not a good idea; they become heavy when wet and take a long time to dry out. Otherwise, it is largely personal choice. Shops will be happy to advise and tempt you, based upon your walking area and the time of year.

Do remember to carry some light **refreshment** as fresh air and exercise can soon make you hungry and thirsty. Be careful about relying too much on the public houses highlighted on the map in rural areas; sadly, many have gone out of business in recent years and despite new licensing laws, many others are not actually open all hours.

By far the most convenient way to carry your food, spare clothes, camera and binoculars, etc, is to stuff everything in a **rucksack**. Modern daysacks, with their broad shoulder straps and clever back designs, can be very comfortable. You can get one for very little outlay. Just put it on your back and forget about it.

Mid winter: look out your gloves, wrap up warm, set a brisk pace, then finish at a pub with a nice log fire.

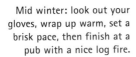

The Secrets of Countryside Access

Steps in the Right Direction

Using the map and following the path

N ow it is time to put our knowledge about paths into practice. Choose a fine day and some agreeable local countryside. Allow yourself plenty of time and don't expect to walk a long way. Some of the route that you are going to follow may not be physically apparent on the ground, especially if the paths are remote or little used. You will need plenty of time to stand and stare at the scenery – and the map.

On the large-scale 1879 map (top), the footpath changes direction slightly where the field is sub-divided.

Start by identifying your position on your 1: 25 000 scale Explorer map   the road junction, station or car park, etc. Then turn to face the road or path that you wish to follow. Next, to **set the map**, hold it flat and turn it so that the route you intend to follow points away from you. What you see ahead of you is also ahead on the map.

On the modern map (above), the surveyor has shown the direct route that walkers take now the hedgerow has been removed. Meanwhile, the definitive path still follows the route our grandparents took.

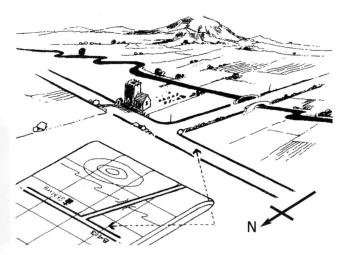

Set the map by turning it so that the direction and/or location of the features shown agree with those around you.

Check your position on the map at each path junction.

Ignore the fact that the names on the map may now be almost upside-down. Just try to ensure that the features on it such as tracks and buildings correspond with those around you. Because north is at the top of the sheet, sometimes the position of the sun can also help you set the map correctly.

Typically, **wayfinding** involves studying each short length of public path as it makes its way in stages across one field and alongside another. Almost every fence or hedge will be defined by a fine black line. Look at the map and see how far ahead you can walk before reaching the next feature, (e.g. field boundary, stream, road, isolated building, path junction) or before there is a definite change of direction. Stop when you get there and check the map again to confirm your new position. Now look around and reorientate your map if necessary. Then repeat the process.

Don't worry if progress seems slow to start with; you are learning to read. If there are lots of paths and fine detail, you will be surprised how often and how closely you have to look at the map. Use a magnifying glass if necessary. Perhaps you will then see that the path makes several small changes of direction before setting off on a certain course. The important thing is to know precisely where you are on the map at all times.

If you are in any doubt, (perhaps there is not a stile in the fence where you expected to find it) refer to the map again to see if all the features around you correspond. Does the map show a wood on the far side of that field? And what about that isolated cottage to the right?

Try and agree on exactly where you are!

Fortunately, we learn by our mistakes, so if you are not sure where you are, it may be wise to return to your previous known position. If you have been looking at the map often enough, that should not be too far. Alternatively, if you can recall the features you have just passed and the twists and turns of the path, it may be possible, by reference to your last known position, to follow on the map the route you have just taken. If it is any consolation, you will probably learn most about wayfinding when you recover from having lost your way.

'To keep the way, or to lose and find it, is one of the great primeval games.'

George Meredith, Hampshire novelist, (1828–1909)

The OS map often gives us more information than we really need, so we are free to choose what is most useful to us in each situation. Usually, we will be referring to the field boundaries or perhaps other tracks, a wood or a river. But where these are sparse or the information appears contradictory, we can call upon the contours (see Chapter 5) to help us decide. Suppose we come to a path junction and it is not obvious which one we should take. Look at the map to see what is different about the two paths. Perhaps one goes up, the other down – or one goes down more steeply than the other.

When a path crosses a large open field with few surrounding features or landmarks, remember to look for any signs or waymarks to supplement the information on the map. Try using your binoculars to see if the next stile or the field exit is visible. Providing the finger post is firm and correctly aligned, it may be possible to set out on the correct cross-field path line by looking back occasionally to see that the finger itself is pointing directly towards you. Alternatively, try lining up an existing field boundary with that shown on the map, so as to establish the angle of your path in relation to it.

Another option, especially useful when a path disappears over the brow of a hill, may be to identify a

Binoculars can be useful to find distant markers and stiles.

Higher paths were often created to avoid a lane that became impassable in winter.

guide feature such as a tall building or pylon on the map or the ground in the distance, that the path appears to be aiming towards. Look up occasionally as you walk so as to check your direction in relation to it.

In this part of the country, we rely heavily on the pattern of **field boundaries** to help us navigate. Walls, fences and hedgerows are all shown simply as fine black detail-lines. If you find yourself confronted by several fences that do not appear on the OS map, perhaps the farmer has strung out some temporary fencing to control grazing animals. Have a look to see how substantial they appear. The surveyor will only include those features that are likely to remain in position for at least 10 years. If there are any hedgerows, concentrate on these as they are likely to be well-established boundaries. They cannot just spring up or be moved overnight.

Sometimes, where a hedge, a fence and a stream, for example, run closely together, only one of these **parallel features** may be shown on our map. For example, a stream could take precedence over the fence/hedge line in black, thus leaving one side of a field defined by a fine blue line.

These walkers have started to follow the sheep track. The footpath actually goes straight ahead alongside the paddock fence.

In the past, many farmers took the opportunity in the name of progress, productivity or profit to remove some of their **hedgerows**. So we may find that some fields are now larger than shown on our map. Since the 1997 Hedgerow Regulations, important hedgerows which (amongst other criteria) include those next to public rights of way, have been given special protection. But **map revision** of such relatively minor detail by the Ordnance Survey has often not kept up with the situation on the ground.

On a map that has been significantly revised, the edition letter will advance; for example from A to B. However, indications are that field boundary changes on Explorer maps are unlikely to be fully revised for some years to come. What we see may be the situation that actually existed on the ground about 30 years ago. Sometimes a clue remains. For example, a line of mature trees or an isolated cattle-trough in the middle of a field could indicate that a boundary has been removed.

Before the hedgerow regulations came into force, some enclosed tracks effectively became headland paths when one side was removed.

Where the green path notation does not stand alone but is actually contained between fine black lines, this tells us that it follows the route of a fenced **track**. If they are broken black lines, look for an unfenced track. (Again, map revision can fail to reflect the tendency for more routes to become fenced in.) Either route should be quite easy to find and to follow, but stay alert; if the next footpath you want is narrow and its existence only betrayed by a small gap in the hedgerow, distracted by good scenery or deep in conversation, it is easy to walk on by.

When it becomes difficult to see the surrounding features, it is easy to lose your way, so you need to be especially vigilant in **woodland**. Look closely to see if

Left turn. Waymarks can help to maintain a single, clearly-defined path through woodland.

Here the footpath crosses a boundary ditch and bank, shown by a black detail-line on the map.

there are any interesting clues on the ground. Did centuries of use create a depression that is now half-buried in leaf-litter perhaps? Or does the path follow an historic bank or ditch that was or still is, a parish or estate boundary, shown on the map. Woodland will often contain tracks used to manage and extract timber that are not actually rights of way. Sometimes the definitive path may be far less significant than these haul-routes which the public may regularly choose instead. Carefully examine the black topographical detail within the green wooded areas on the map for clues. Think about referring to the contours if necessary.

Indefinite detail is not surveyed precisely. This applies particularly to **vegetation** such as scrub, bracken and patches of coppice woodland, etc., where the boundaries are often vague and sometimes seasonal. Similarly, the position and number of individual or scattered tree symbols should be considered representative and not specific. Experience will enable you to appreciate the limitations of scale.

The tall **pylons** that carry overhead power lines may not be a particularly attractive feature, but they can sometimes help with navigation. Bear in mind that only the more conspicuous may be shown on our map and the smaller pylons omitted where detail is crowded. Trees have to be removed where transmission lines pass over woodland and unfortunately, locals often use these ample clearings at the expense of rights of way nearby, which may be overgrown and difficult to find. Buildings such as **churches** that have a tower, spire, dome or minaret and that are no longer used for worship will continue to be shown on the map because they are an important navigational feature.

By all means keep a simple **compass** in your rucksack
so that if you come for example to a large freshly-
cultivated field where the path has not yet been
reinstated and there are no waymarks to direct you or
guide-features to aim for, you will be able to orientate
the map correctly and head approximately in the right
direction. Alternatively, if there are just too many paths
to choose from (on open heathland perhaps) or you have
become confused and disorientated by following
countless small woodland paths, you will at least be able
to know the best course to follow. As soon as you come
to a recognisable feature, look for it on the map and
continue as before.

Although no longer used as
a chapel, the spire is a
landmark for a map-reader.

Some readers may be disappointed that we have not
devoted a whole chapter on how to use a compass in this
booklet. Fortunately, walkers do not need to be an expert
on this subject to be able to explore the patchwork of
countryside that constitutes most of south-east England.
A compass is a magnetic device, not a magic one. Do not
expect it to tell you where you are on the map; to do
that, you will need to take and plot bearings from at
least two distant and identifiable features.

A free leaflet published by the Ordnance Survey
called *'Advanced map reading made easy'* is devoted
almost exclusively to using a compass. Alternatively, you
could take comedian (and RA vice-President) Mike
Harding's advice (*Rambling On*, Guild Publishing 1986)
and navigate using a ball of string! Just post the string to
where you want to go, the summit of Scafell Pike for
instance, keeping hold of the other end of the string. All
you have to do then is follow the string from your house
to the top of Scafell, winding it up as you go along.

Currently this footpath
alongside the River Thames
ends at the well-worn post
where the ferry used to tie up.

Path Practice

Look at the following examples of a path going for nearly 5 kilometres (about 3 miles) through the countryside:

- Strip map **A** (left) shows an imaginary Explorer map, turned so that our chosen route (highlighted in yellow) stretches out before us.

- Map **B** (opposite page) shows how to follow this path in simple stages, *without* reference to the contours.

- Map **C** (opposite page) shows how to follow this same path using *just* the contours and the water courses.
  See page 35 for a contour model of this strip map.

MAP A

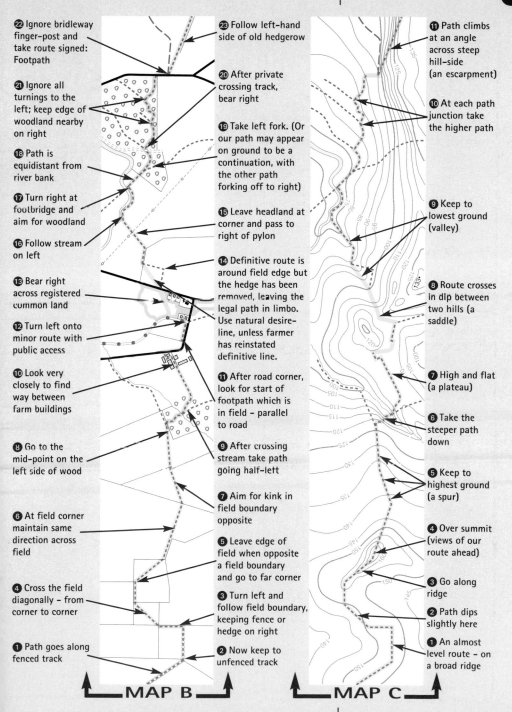

MAP B

㉒ Ignore bridleway finger-post and take route signed: Footpath

㉑ Ignore all turnings to the left; keep edge of woodland nearby on right

⑱ Path is equidistant from river bank

⑰ Turn right at footbridge and aim for woodland

⑯ Follow stream on left

⑬ Bear right across registered common land

⑫ Turn left onto minor route with public access

⑩ Look very closely to find way between farm buildings

⑧ Go to the mid-point on the left side of wood

⑥ At field corner maintain same direction across field

④ Cross the field diagonally – from corner to corner

① Path goes along fenced track

㉓ Follow left-hand side of old hedgerow

⑳ After private crossing track, bear right

⑲ Take left fork. (Or our path may appear on ground to be a continuation, with the other path forking off to right)

⑮ Leave headland at corner and pass to right of pylon

⑭ Definitive route is around field edge but the hedge has been removed, leaving the legal path in limbo. Use natural desire-line, unless farmer has reinstated definitive line.

⑪ After road corner, look for start of footpath which is in field – parallel to road

⑨ After crossing stream take path going half-left

⑦ Aim for kink in field boundary opposite

⑤ Leave edge of field when opposite a field boundary and go to far corner

③ Turn left and follow field boundary, keeping fence or hedge on right

② Now keep to unfenced track

MAP C

⑪ Path climbs at an angle across steep hill-side (an escarpment)

⑩ At each path junction take the higher path

⑨ Keep to lowest ground (valley)

⑧ Route crosses in dip between two hills (a saddle)

⑦ High and flat (a plateau)

⑥ Take the steeper path down

⑤ Keep to highest ground (a spur)

④ Over summit (views of our route ahead)

③ Go along ridge

② Path dips slightly here

① An almost level route – on a broad ridge

4

Reviewing the evidence
Some path issues and anomalies explained

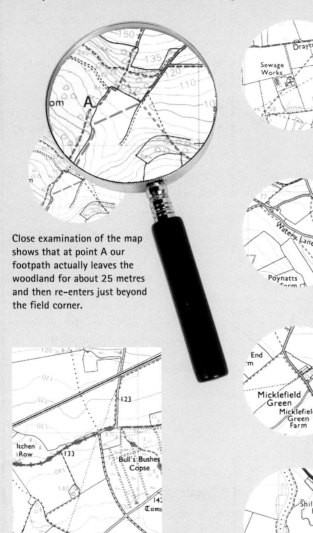

Close examination of the map shows that at point A our footpath actually leaves the woodland for about 25 metres and then re-enters just beyond the field corner.

The fine, black, pecked line shows that the original path was direct. But following a diversion, walkers are now obliged to zig-zag around several field edges.

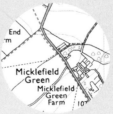

Approval for this sewage works was given without taking the right of way into account. The OS will only amend the definitive map when they receive information from the Highway Authority that the path has been legally diverted.

The road name here gives a clue as to the origin of the parallel footpath.

Footpaths alongside roads can easily go unnoticed on the map. This one is the result of two path diversions.

These dead-end paths are the result of a missing ferry – and the failure of the path to be claimed in the adjoining parish.

The surveyor has shown the straight line now used and reinstated on the ground. But the green, definitive path still follows the route alongside old field boundaries and hedgerows, since removed.

Unfortunately. the desire-line direct to Aldermaston church was officially diverted in 1956 (without any objections being received), thereby forcing walkers to use what is now a very busy road.

The broken green line follows the route taken in 1949. But today the layout of the drive follows a slightly different alignment, with the result that our path appears to cross into the field for no apparent reason.

Cul-de-sac paths can be quite legitimate. Here are two examples; one to the hilltop and the other to the village well.

Planning a Walk

Here are a few ideas that you might like to take into account when planning a walk, particularly if there are likely to be quite a few in the party.

- High on the list of priorities has to be **safety**, such as choosing the best direction for any unavoidable lengths of road-walking or sight-lines at road crossings.
- Unless you plan to maintain the elevation, on a circular walk, resist the temptation to choose a **high starting point** with a marvellous view. Folk will not be too enthusiastic about climbing back to the finish when they are tired and have already admired the scene.
- Try to ensure plenty of **variety** and, if you can include a focal point, that will help to give the walk extra purpose.
- A local **guidebook** or map can be useful to find starting places where you can leave cars, some concessionary paths that have only been promoted locally and also perhaps some local history.

75584

Lie of the Land
The value of contours

The closer the contours, the steeper the climb.

This is what contours would look like if they were actually drawn on the ground. (The Holies, National Trust access land near Streatley, Berkshire)

A s we have seen, in most circumstances we navigate simply by reference to the roads, fields, rivers, woods and all the other features that we see around us. But as walkers, our focus will invariably be drawn to the natural lie of the land: to its folds, undulations and, in particular, to the high ground and hilltops. We can also use this aspect to help us find our way.

Since our map is only a flat sheet of paper, this third dimension is presented to us in the form of **contour lines**. (See strip map C, page 29.) These fine brown lines

on our map are plotted by joining together points of the same height above sea level. We can use this extra information when there is little else to guide us, or perhaps when there are so many paths that it is difficult to make the right choice. Contours represent one of the few aspects of our landscape that has changed very little over the centuries.

Although it is always interesting to know the actual height above sea level of a particular viewpoint, what effectively makes the countryside hilly and the paths steep to walk is the difference in height between one piece of land and another. So, if there are lots of contour lines drawn on the map where we plan to walk, then it is liable to be quite strenuous. Conversely, if there are none

or very few, we can identify the land as relatively flat, even though it may be high ground (a plateau).

Because a contour line joins points of equal height, if our path follows a contour line it must be level. Similarly, if the path is equidistant between two contours, it is also going to be virtually level.

If our route gets closer or actually crosses a contour line, it must be either going up towards the next contour height or down towards the contour below. To answer this uncertainty, we need to find an area nearby on the map where the height of some contours is given. A feature of these values is that they are always positioned so as to read correctly when facing up hill. Alternatively, you might check the immediate area for rivers, lakes or streams as these will always be at the lower points. Either method will enable you to decide if the value of subsequent contour lines will be getting higher or lower. To help us further, significant contours with for example 25, 50 and 75 metre values, etc. are drawn as a thicker line.

Every time you reach another contour line on the Explorer map, you will have either climbed or descended five metres. So the more frequently you cross them (i.e. the closer together they are), the steeper the slope. In mountainous areas this vertical interval is increased to every ten metres to avoid them being too close to each other.

Probably the most common fault lies in misreading the situation; what you thought was *up* hill is actually going down. This is often the result of a superficial glance at the map. **Spot heights** can sometimes help. Surveyors generally take heights along roads where they rise or fall, at valley junctions and, of course, at high points and on hilltops. The most prominent of these may also feature a **trig** (*triangulation*) point on the summit, shown on our map as a small blue triangle. Although often indicative of a panoramic view, there may not necessarily be any public access to these concrete pillars. Global positioning satellites have made them redundant for their original mapping purpose.

Next time you find yourself admiring a fine view, take the opportunity to compare the scene beyond with the contours on the map. Do not expect every rise in the ground to influence the line; a small mound will need to be at least five metres high if it is to appear – about equal to the height of the guttering on a normal house.

Study the contours on a map and with practice, you may find that you can actually create in your own mind an intriguing model of the landscape.

Not all trig pillars are accessible from a public right of way.

A contour model of strip map C shown on page 29.

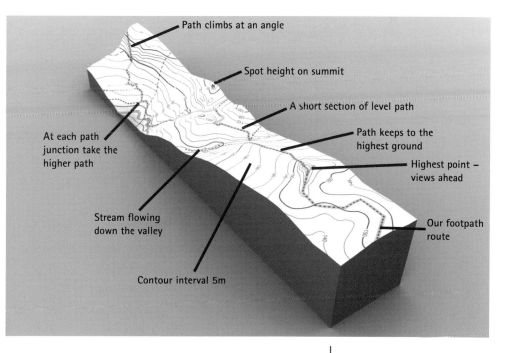

Path climbs at an angle

Spot height on summit

A short section of level path

Path keeps to the highest ground

Highest point – views ahead

At each path junction take the higher path

Our footpath route

Stream flowing down the valley

Contour interval 5m

Time and Pace

Measuring distance, estimating time

Driving a car enables most of us if we so choose, to be almost instantly somewhere else, and with very little effort. But, for a walk, we really do need to have some idea how long it will take us to cover the distance between two places on the map. Everybody has their favourite method. Here are a few suggestions to get you started.

To avoid confusion, always use the same scale of map for country walking, preferably the Explorer sheet. All OS maps are now based on a **metric scale**. The evidence for this is perhaps most clearly illustrated by the spacing of the grid lines across the face of the map. On all OS maps, the **grid lines** are one kilometre apart. At our 1: 2 5,000 scale, one kilometre is represented by four centimetres on the map. A rough estimate of distance can therefore be gleaned by simply counting the number of grid squares through which our route passes and treating any path which goes diagonally across a square as about 1.5 km in length. This method can be particularly useful out in the field and will give you the distance in kilometres.

Unfortunately, the Metrication Board set up by the government in 1969 failed to complete the job of conversion, so we have the rather incongruous situation of metric weights, measures and maps, but speed limits, fuel consumption and road direction signs, etc. still in miles. If you wish to convert kilometres to miles, the simplest way is to multiply by six and divide by ten

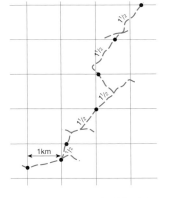

Using the OS grid to estimate the length of a route in kilometres.

The Secrets of Countryside Access

(i.e. move the decimal point one place), then round it up a bit. So, for example, 8 km x 6 = 48; divide by 10 = 4.8 and call it 5 miles. Actually, it is 4.97 miles.

For those who would rather think directly in imperial measurements, the scale of our map is about 2½ inches to one mile. A good way to take some of the guesswork out of trying to estimate this length is to prepare a piece of string marked or knotted every 2½ inches and lay it along the route. It's fiddly, but this will immediately give you an approximate distance in miles. Some folk may laugh, but there is no investment and no batteries to replace.

To measure any distance more accurately, the most satisfactory method is to invest in a map measurer. With the sheet spread out on a firm, flat surface, carefully run the small wheel along the route, then read off the distance on the dial according to the scale of the map;

or, if you prefer, run it off along the scale bar at the bottom of the map. Like most things, there is now a computer programme available to do the job, perhaps more accurately but more expensively.

Experience indicates that in normal circumstances, a walker out for the day in the lowlands will average about 2 miles (3.25 kilometres) an hour. On shorter journeys without a stop for lunch, this could be 2½ miles (4 kilometres) an hour. Physical fitness, the gradient, the weather, the surface underfoot or even the number of stiles and the number of people in the group can play their part. Be ready for all these elements to combine if you have a bus or train to catch!

Some other guidelines:

Allow 12 minutes for one kilometre on a road or metalled surface,15 minutes on a track and 20 minutes on a field-path, or more if it goes up hill or you are unfortunate enough to find it freshly ploughed. Adjust these times to suit your own abilities, or the least able in your group.

'After a day's walk everything has twice the usual value.'

George Macaulay Trevelyan, English and walking essayist, (1876–1962)

Pinpoint Positioning
Using the grid reference system

How can you immediately locate somewhere that is out in the country, literally in the middle of nowhere? Don't waste your time with road names and detailed route directions; the easiest way to find the start of that country walk for example is to plot the **grid reference**.

Unfortunately, the sight of a full grid reference value such as SU 561807 can horrify many people. But you do not need any qualifications to crack this code. The principle is very simple.

This small diagram has been sub-divided by a series of vertical and horizontal lines so as to form a grid and make a number of small squares within. They have been numbered A, B, C, D along the bottom and 1, 2, 3, 4 up the side. If you thought the red square was at D2, you would be right. This is a simple form of grid reference to identify that square.

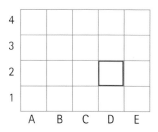

The same principle applies on our Ordnance Survey Explorer map, which has a series of fine, blue, vertical and horizontal lines drawn across it to form the grid. Each line is numbered in the border around the edge of the map. They are also repeated across the centre of the map face for convenience when the map is being used partially folded.

Let us assume the start for a walk is given as 764738. This is a six-figure grid reference and quite sufficient for most purposes. It is actually made up of two groups of three numbers. The first three are **Eastings** and the last three are **Northings**. So we have 764 *east* and 738 *north*.

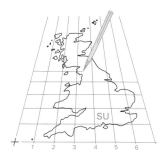

Starting from the SW corner, the country was divided up by drawing a series of vertical lines (Eastings) and then horizontal lines (Northings) to create a grid of squares.

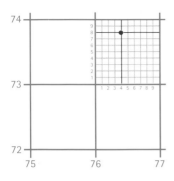

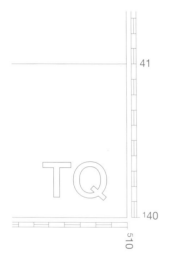

Corner of an OS sheet
showing sub-divisions
and the prefix.

The Eastings are the large numbers along the bottom of the sheet. They start on the left and read along towards the right or *east* side of the map. The Northings are the large numbers up the side of the sheet. They start at the bottom and read up towards the top or *north* of the map. Use the following to help you remember the sequence: *Go along the hall, then go up the stairs.* So, to plot this position, we first need to look for the large number 76 along the bottom and then the number 73 up the side of the map. From these four figures, we have been able to identify the grid square that contains our position.

To find our location within this square it is usually sufficient to simply estimate the extra four tenths (76**4**) of the distance between the grid lines going east and then additional eight tenths (73**8**) north. If you wish to do this precisely, look closely at the way the lines have been drawn in the map border and you will see that it has actually been subdivided into ten divisions between each of the grid values. You can use these sub-divisions to find where to draw one line up and another line across the map. Our grid reference point is situated at the intersection of these two lines.

Providing our area of concern is sufficiently restricted, it is quite normal for the prefix letters to be ignored, as we have done. However, with the letters SU for example, added, our original six-figure grid reference does become totally unique. If you wanted to give a friend the location of somewhere in another part of the country, it would be important to include the correct prefix. The grid letters that cover the sheet are shown in the legend. In practice, most people find that it is easier to simply refer to the name or number of the relevant Explorer sheet instead. The grid reference explained above, for example, actually identifies the approximate position of my house on the Reading map, sheet number 159.

In the legend, you will also find an example of how to *record* a grid reference point. You will notice this is just the same procedure in reverse. If, for example, you want to report a path problem to a rights of way officer or meet a friend for a walk, it is useful to be able to quote the grid reference, so that he or she can find the exact position easily.

Take time to compare the detail on the map with the features around you.

A Power and a Duty
The Highway Authorities' responsibilities

All public rights of way should be signposted where they leave a metalled road.

It is the statutory duty of the county councils (and unitary authorities) as the Highway Authorities, to assert and protect the rights of the public to the use and enjoyment of all the public rights of way in their area. They also have various discretionary powers to help users and to carry out improvements.

It is the starting point for a host of country delights and an important requirement of the Highway Authority that every public right of way should have a **signpost** where it leaves the metalled road. Without it, some paths might remain almost undiscovered. The post will be at the start of the path and the finger should indicate the initial direction of the path. Very occasionally, it may be positioned on the opposite side of the road. This may be done so as to avoid the post being knocked over – or perhaps as a rather discreet way of indicating a path which is also a private drive.

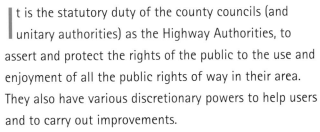

Look out for those situations where the finger-post has been positioned on the opposite side of the road.

The finger will also classify the route as either a footpath, bridleway or byway, etc. In Oxfordshire, it may also give you a destination and a distance, as indeed some old signs did here long ago. Occasionally, the definitive path number may also have been added, usually by the parish or a voluntary footpath warden.

Footpath Waymark

You may also find signposts erected at some non-roadside locations, for example on popular routes or at complicated path junctions. Otherwise the way should be indicated if necessary by using a **waymark**. This arrow can take many different forms. Initially in Berkshire and South Oxfordshire, a system of painted white arrows was agreed. Many of these are still doing good service and will be found on stiles and trees throughout Berkshire and the Chilterns. They do have the advantage that they can be individually shaped to suit particular circumstances and will not damage a tree.

Bridleway Waymark

However, it is now more likely that you will see white plastic discs (or green metal plates in Hampshire) that have been provided by the Highway Authority in consultation with the landowner. It may be on a post erected for the purpose. They show the status of the route by using one of the Countryside Agency colour-coded arrows; Yellow indicates a Footpath, Blue a Bridleway and Red a Byway. Any Permitted Paths will be identified as such and usually marked in Berkshire by a white arrow on a green disc.

At a crossing path. To avoid confusion, view waymarks as you approach them.

All waymarks should be positioned so that they appear directly in front of the user, similar to normal road signs. Where a path turns left or right just beyond a feature to which a waymark has been added, the Countryside Agency arrowhead is not always adequate

Path turns left, alongside fence   Path is on other side of the fence

Which side of the fence should
you be on? Use of the straight
and bent waymark-arrow.

and the tail needs to be extended and bent for it to be
clear. To get the best indication of the route ahead, view
the waymark from the path as you approach it. Some are
not very accurate, so check with the map if in doubt. If
the waymark is on a stile, remember to refer to it before
you climb over.

All land is owned by someone, so every road and path
is over someone's land. Even where the title deeds
include this land, the **surface** of the way and a few
inches of subsoil are vested in the authority. This is
necessary for the protection and maintenance of the

The Highway Authority is
responsible for the surface of all
public rights of way.

Byway resurfacing works being
carried out by the Highway
Authority, using a permeable
membrane and road scalpings.

highway, including the control of **undergrowth**; that is to say, the natural vegetation growing upon it. The majority of local authorities in this area operate a regular programme of spring and summer clearance of those paths that get reported to them. Fenced paths can be especially prone to summer growth and are more difficult to maintain.

Highway Authority responsibilities also includes **drainage** and surfacing works. If the surface is constantly being damaged by other users, it may be possible, if there is sufficient width, to segregate walkers by erecting posts or similar. Inappropriate use by motor bikes and heavy vehicles can create serious damage and repairs often put considerable financial pressure on the budget of local councils for rights of way. In these circumstances, the authorities, who are responsible for ensuring that use is regulated and not inappropriate, may try to encourage voluntary restraint.

If this fails, a **Traffic Regulation Order** (TRO) can be imposed. A permanent order may be used to restrict or prohibit motor traffic on a byway, for example. Or a temporary TRO could be applied for a period of up to six months to a route which might otherwise be seriously damaged or so that work can be carried out.

Because streams and rivers, slopes and ridges are natural features that hinder or obstruct users of a highway, it is the responsibility of the authority to overcome them if necessary or desirable, by providing and maintaining **footbridges**, steps, embankments, boardwalks and other works. Where they also serve the farmer or are privately owned, costs may be shared. If a bridge is the means by which a path crosses a man-made

Report surface growth to the council so that it can be included in their regular summer clearance programme.

It is an offence to damage the surface of the highway.

Most footbridges are the responsibility of the Highway Authority.

A footbridge will be provided if it is considered necessary or desirable. Therefore, only paths in remote, mountainous areas are likely to offer walkers a challenge.

A good 2.5-metre-wide fenced path. All orders for new or diverted paths must now include a statement of width.

obstacle such as a railway, canal or ditch, then the railway, canal authority, farmer or landowner is most likely responsible.

To be convenient, a path also needs to have sufficient usable **width** for users to pass each other. The law does set minimum widths for paths through crops, *(See chapter 10)* but elsewhere it is not so precise. The Highway Authority can enforce a path width if it is given in the definitive statement, and probably also if evidence such as large-scale maps or past practice indicate that historically the public's rights of passage are not so limited. Stiles, gates and footbridges are limitations that need approval and should not be taken as an indication of the path width elsewhere.

If you find a riverside path getting washed away due to **erosion**, the authority needs to be alerted so that they can take the necessary steps to re-establish it. If it should totally disappear (as in the case of a cliff-top path that suddenly falls into the sea), the authority or landowner may claim that the path has ceased to exist.

Temporary repair to a riverside path by RA club members.

This highway verge, unlawfully planted with holly, is putting walkers at unnecessary risk. Removed following a complaint.

In these days of fast moving traffic, road-side **verges** can be very important to walkers and to riders. Historically they are as much an integral part of the highway as the metalled surface itself and need to be safeguarded from illegal attempts to obstruct or encroach upon them. The owner of any adjoining property will need a licence from the Highway Authority if he wishes to plant or maintain it.

Highway Authorities can also make **improvements** to existing highways and may be persuaded to construct board-walks and steps, etc. Many simple pro-walking measures can be implemented at very little cost, for

If there is sufficient width, it is sometimes possible to segregate users on a byway or a bridleway.

Here a bridleway and a footpath have been created separately on land formally used for gravel extraction.

Surface improvements; a flight of steps and a board-walk over wet, low-lying ground.

Above left and above.
Improving walkers safety.

example, safety barriers and signs advising motorists that people may be crossing or walking in the road. Bollards can be erected and footways marked out so as to protect or define the surface for otherwise vulnerable walkers.

There is no reason why specific requests, such as practical alternatives to using busy roads, links in the path network or between settlements and elsewhere, should not be considered. (See also Rights of Way Improvement Plans, page 66.) Local authorities have the power to make **creation agreements**, or **creation orders** if it is considered that this would add to the convenience or enjoyment of a substantial section of the public.

It is also an important duty of the Highway Authority to keep the definitive map under continuous review. **Modification orders** need to be made whenever a path is diverted or extinguished (see Chapter 10) so that the map can reflect the legal changes made to the network. This information is then used by the Ordnance Survey, as the national mapping agency, to update the maps we use.

Modification orders that propose to correct an error, add an unrecorded way or create a new path will be advertised so that representations or objections can be made and, if necessary, considered by the Secretary of State.

An example of a path creation order made by the local authority. Following pressure from RA, country walkers can now avoid a busy dual carriageway near Marlow, by using an existing archway.

Respect for Public Rights
The owners' and occupiers' responsibilities

It is important that farmers and landowners know where footpaths and bridleways cross their land and treat them with respect. Well kept, easy-to-follow rights of way reduce the problems and annoyance associated with accidental trespass and can only help improve the farming industry's image.

To manage their land effectively, especially for livestock, farmers need to erect fences and preserve hedgerows. So it is primarily the owner's responsibility to avoid obstructing the public's right of way by providing and maintaining stiles, gates and similar structures at these points. Landownes may claim 25% of their costs of maintenance and repair from the Highway Authorities, but must get prior written approval from the council for any **new structure** that they wish to erect across a right of way.

A farmer repairing the stile in his fence.
Photo: ©Stuart Shurlock

Wooden **stiles** are still common throughout the area, but many are below an acceptable standard. If not simply dilapidated, the most common fault is for the step to be too high. The British Standard recommends a maximum height of only about 12 inches. (That's well below your knee.) The step itself should also be wide enough and not rest upon a cross-member or it will soon rock back and forth. A hand-post and second step are frequently needed. However, stiles are often unnecessary where land is now arable or where the path itself has been fenced in. It is estimated that about half the population find stiles difficult to use.

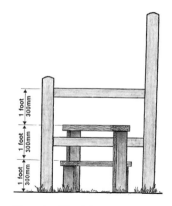

Steps should not be more than a foot high.

Each step should be broad and flat. Adding a few u-nails or a rigid wire-mesh will avoid them from becoming slippery.

Stuck on a stile; even good stiles can act as a barrier to walkers later in life. Mrs Ramm, née Stanford, in 1926 and 1986.

The kissing gate. Kids score five points for each one in their I Spy book!

Trying out a less restrictive version of the traditional kissing gate.

Whenever the opportunity arises, stiles should be removed or replaced with pedestrian **gates** so as to follow the code of practice set out in the Disability Discrimination Act, 1995. When old stiles need to be replaced, a new fence is erected or a new route created, perhaps as a result of a diversion, the least restrictive option should be chosen. Kissing gates, so called because the gate simply touches or 'kisses' the hoop – *(you might prefer to keep this morsel from your beloved)* – and self-closing pedestrian gates are easier to negotiate, particularly for the elderly and less able. Councils appear more likely to help fund these where routes are promoted or close to towns and villages.

A self-closing gate; especially suitable between one field and the next.

Kissing gate for the disabled; wheelchair users undo the padlock, walkers use it in the normal way.

> In its constitution, the Ramblers' aim to encourage all persons to enjoy the countryside, including those with limited mobility.
>
> Disabled ramblers using manually operated or battery-powered wheelchairs, which can operate at 4mph, are legally classified as pedestrians. Self-closing gates with specialised latches, and kissing gates that can be fully opened, wide enough for wheelchair users to pass through, can help them to access some interesting routes such as the Thames Path between Maidenhead and Windsor.

Centrewire©

Walkers are sometimes confused by the presence of a padlock on some new kissing gates. These gates are specially designed to enable wheelchair users, who are issued with a RADAR key, to pass through. Walkers use them in the normal way.

A number of 'V' shaped **squeeze stiles** were supplied over the years by the old Berkshire County Council, especially in the western half of the county. Sometimes there may be a cross-bar to lift. These non-climbing structures are cheaper and quicker to install, but some farmers consider them unsuitable where there is livestock, particularly lambs. In the parishes around Bracknell, the 'Rambler' self-closing pedestrian gates were erected. Hold the two pivot posts apart and step through.

In many arable areas where there is no livestock to be contained, no structure may be needed. In these circumstances, it should be quite acceptable for there to be simply a **gap**, providing it is not necessary to restrict other users. However, it can often be useful to provide a waymark here so walkers feel confident that they are on

A squeeze stile

Often a gap is all that is required – especially between arable fields.

The self-closing 'Rambler' stile.

Gates on bridleways; the tall handle allows riders to open them without having to dismount.

the path. Alternatively, a simple staggered barrier or **stile-way** may be constructed that only requires a slight zig-zag movement by walkers, but is usually sufficient to restrict horses and cyclists.

The tall raised handle on a self-closing **bridle-gate** enables it to be opened by a rider on horse-back. Sometimes walkers and riders will be expected to use the farmer's existing **field-gate**, which should be easy to

open. If it is not, or you are not sure that you will be able to fasten the gate afterwards and have no alternative but to climb over, choose the hinged end and report as an obstruction. There is no requirement for stiles to be suitable for dogs, but enlightened landowners may occasionally provide a **dog latch**, although of course any type of gate would immediately give unbridled passage for his master too.

The dog latch

Tell the Highway Authority if you are unable to use the full width of a path.

Landowners are also responsible for keeping paths clear of **overhanging growth** in exactly the same way that a home owner is required to keep his hedge from spilling out onto the pavement. This can be a particular problem for walkers when the path width is already restricted, perhaps between fences. If a tree falls across the path, again the owner is obliged to remove it, although the county field-officer may be persuaded to arrange for his rights of way team to clear sufficient to allow free passage.

As a concession granted after the war, farmers are allowed to **plough** or otherwise disturb a cross-field footpath or bridleway (if not easily avoided), provided that the surface is made good within 24 hours or a

Cross-fields paths must not be ploughed up if they can be avoided.

9

After the first disturbance of the soil for any particular crop, farmers are allowed a maximum of two weeks in which to reinstate the path.

After this further disturbance of the soil, the path must be reinstated within 24 hours.

Fine soil and a freshly-defined path between Upper and Lower Wield in Hampshire.

maximum of two weeks if this is the first such disturbance for this particular crop. **Reinstatement** of the path is best carried out immediately the work is completed. It must be made reasonably convenient to use with the line of the path clearly apparent on the ground at all times. This is often done by running the tractor wheels along it, or occasionally by putting a line of markers in the ground. Any path that weaves a crooked line across an arable field was probably not reinstated but actually created by walkers coming from both directions trying to find their own way.

Although the farmer may initially disturb the surface of a footpath or bridleway that crosses a field, under the 1990 Rights of Way Act he must not allow any **crop**

obstruction of the path, other than grass. The best option is to avoid sowing a crop on the line of the path. However, if the farmer cannot manage to do this, he will need to use some mechanical or chemical method to keep the way convenient to use. Some crops such as oil-seed rape and broad beans will collapse and obstruct a path unless sufficient width is allowed by the farmer at the outset, or the growing crop is kept trimmed back to avoid making the path difficult to use.

The farmer is obliged to maintain the following minimum **path widths** through the crop:

cross-field footpath – 1 metre

field-edge footpath – 1.5 metres

cross-field bridleway – 2 metres

field-edge bridleway (and any other unsurfaced highway) – 3 metres.

Failure to comply is an offence and, if necessary, the Highway Authority can cut the crop and send the owner the bill.

A field–path must be kept clear of standing crops at all times.

The perfect target for farmers (and walkers) – if there is a big field to cross.

Marking the line of a public footpath by using the tractor wheels.

Headland paths must not be ploughed.

There is no requirement for the surface of a cross-field bridleway to be especially suitable for cyclists.

It is unlawful to plough any right of way that runs along the side or **headland** of a field. The word comes from the term *head land*, given to the land around the edge of the field, formerly needed for turning the plough. Before the hedgerow regulations came into force, some field-edge paths were also effectively created by removing the hedge from one side of a track, thus leaving it open to the field. Some mid-field paths that the owner must now reinstate, would also originally have been alongside a hedge.

The surface of any route over which the public may have vehicular rights, including roads used as public paths and byways open to all traffic, should never be disturbed, of course.

Speaking up for Footpaths
Threats, changes and improvements

Much of the appeal inherent in our country paths, lies in their originally created from – and although there will always be development and change, if the integrity of the network is to be maintained walkers need to be vigilant and authorities sensitive to this. Everyone who lives or walks in the country should be able to find them, enjoy them and know what they can do to help safeguard them.

If a Highway Authority receives an application to permanently move or **divert** a right of way, the council is not legally obliged to process it. Although it does have the power to do so and it should examine and give due consideration to the proposal, it is not duty-bound to publish an Order. The CRoW Act, 2000 will give an applicant the right of appeal against non-determination of an order by the Authority if he considers that he has been in some way discriminated against.

Paths often come under threat when a new owner buys a property and then takes exception to walkers crossing his land. He may own the land, but he cannot own a right *that belongs to the public.* However, an application to have it diverted or even extinguished could be submitted. Elsewhere, a farmer who has been obstructing a path with crops for many years perhaps, when asked by the Highway Authority to reinstate the path, may be prompted to seek for a diversion around the field edges.

For an application to be approved, the council needs to be satisfied that it is in the interests of the owner of

'A lot of the walking public is apathetic because they accept deferentially the paths given them, rather than seeing them as precious, imperilled rights to be defended.'

Chris Hall, Editor of The Countryman (1981–96)

A diversion order notice must be displayed at each end of the path.

the land or of the public (or both) that the path be diverted. But the new route must also not be substantially less convenient to the public and councillors must have regard to the effect of the diversion on public enjoyment of the way as a whole. Authorities will consult user groups such as the RA and Open Spaces Society, and the British Horse Society if a bridleway is involved before proceeding further. Perhaps a compromise can be reached.

When people read that a council has 'made an order', they often assume that a decision has been taken and that it is already too late to do anything about it. But in this context it is important to understand that 'made' simply means that the authority has initiated the procedure. The path cannot be moved unless or until, the order is subsequently **confirmed**. A plan and a copy of the order notice must be displayed on the path at either end of the proposed diversion and a notice published in at least one local newspaper. Look under the heading 'Public Notices' (see page 92). Ask yourself which route you would prefer. Perhaps the alternative is longer and less direct, steeper or more difficult to walk. Which path has the better view? Anyone who considers that an application is not well-founded may object to it within the 28-day period allowed. Don't always leave it to someone else; if it is not in the walkers' interest for the path to be moved, object. Sometimes it only takes one person to save a path.

If there are no objections, the council can confirm the order. However, if any member of the public considers that some (or all) of the criteria have not been met, they can and should object to it. In these circumstances, the council

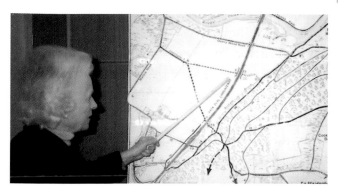

Presenting the ramblers' case at a public inquiry.

can either withdraw or pass the order to the Secretary of State, who may deal with it by written representations or a hearing if objectors agree, or by calling a local **public inquiry**. In this latter case, anyone who has not previously responded can be invited to express their opinion. This is a good opportunity for those who feel aggrieved but missed the statutory deadline for objections.

After considering all the evidence, the inspector will then recommend that the Secretary of State should either confirm or reject the application. As you will appreciate, this procedure can be complicated, expensive and time-consuming for everyone concerned. If a diversion is approved, the new path must be in a fit condition for use before the existing path can be closed.

It is helpful if diversions are indicated on the ground until revised maps are available.

DAVID WILSON HOMES

WE APOLOGISE FOR ANY INCONVENIENCE CAUSED DURING THE PROGRESS OF THESE WORKS

FOOTPATH CLOSED

Temporary closure orders can be made for up to six months at a time.

The original width of this byway has been reduced by the erection of a new fence. A request for enforcement action has been made.

Property owners cannot simply take part of the public highway for their own use. New fencing reported and moved back.

It is then good practice for an **official notice** to be displayed at both ends of the old path, giving clear directions on how to find the new route. This should remain in place until all the maps and guidebooks of the area have been updated.

Walkers should oppose all applications to close, stop-up or **extinguish** a right of way unless the path is genuinely not needed for public use, either now or in the future.

Keep a look out for attempts to **encroach** upon the original width of a path. The right of way is the whole width between the original boundaries, not just that trodden down the centre! Property owners often attempt this in stages to gain a few extra inches at the expense of the public, one new fence replacing another or beyond an overgrown hedge. If possible, report attempts to reduce the width of a path before it becomes established. Unfortunately, at the present time there is otherwise no statutory minimum width for a path that is or becomes enclosed between fences or hedges.

Existing public rights of way need to be taken into account before development begins.

District councils and Unitary authorities are the planning authorities and they should check planning applications to see if any rights of way are affected by proposed **development**. Diversion and extinguishment orders may be authorised under the Town & Country Planning Act 1990, providing it is necessary (not simply convenient or expedient from the developer's point of view) to enable the development to take place.

If an extinguishment is proposed, we need to ask ourselves if the path could be diverted instead. Consultations should be undertaken with parish councils and user groups. Notices must be displayed and publicity given so that anyone concerned about the effect on the path can make representations to the planning authority. In the past, authorities have often been guilty of ignoring these procedures and, as a result, users will sometimes find recent development shown on the map that completely ignores existing rights-of-way. (see example on page 30)

Even if planning permission is granted, this does not give the developer the right to interfere with or block the way until such time as an order has been made and confirmed. On new housing estates, existing rights of way are best incorporated into broad, attractive and

When development took place here the original path-alignment was retained and enhanced.

A permissive path can be useful, providing it is not a substitute for an existing footpath.

user-friendly **greenways**, rather than extinguished or pushed into narrow passages between houses. A number of useful new paths have also been created in recent years as a result of what is popularly known as **planning gain**. Extra routes can sometimes result from negotiations by the planning authority, who are obliged to seek improvements from developers to counter the impact of proposals to build, extract gravel or to make a change-of-use, such as a golf course.

Parish councils also have some powers relating to rights of way within their parish, including the right to prosecute anyone who wilfully obstructs free passage, or a farmer who does not restore a path after ploughing or allows his crops to inconvenience users. How willing they may be to actually exercise this power sometimes depends on the persuasion of the councillors, who are themselves often drawn from the local farming community. However parish councils are well placed, and should be encouraged to make improvements and promote the use of their paths, starting perhaps with some of those closest to the village itself.

Some enlightened parish councils offer one or two kissing gates each year to encourage more use of their paths.

From time to time, as a result of various national schemes and local authority funding, resources and help are available to enable **volunteer groups** to undertake projects in their area. Over the years, improvements and promotion of the paths by knowledgeable organisations and enthusiastic individuals, working on behalf of the Highway Authority, have helped to open up and restore many paths across the region and encourage their use.

Study any large-scale map and you often find other routes, generally referred to as **'lost ways'**, which were not marked on the definitive map in 1949. If a path stops at the parish boundary, for example, it is an indication that no one checked to see that it was also being claimed in the adjoining parish. Until recently, the maxim *'once a highway, always a highway'* meant that claims based upon historical evidence could be brought forward despite more recent developments on the ground. As if to draw a line under this situation, recent legislation has set the year 2026 as the cut-off date for registering all these historical rights on the basis of pre-1949 documentary evidence.

Also if you know of some paths that the public already use but which are not actually rights of way (and therefore do not enjoy the same protection), you can make an application to the local authority to have this **unrecorded way** added to the definitive map. Providing it can be shown that the public have used a way for an uninterrupted period of 20 years or more 'as of right', anyone can submit a **claim** for that route to be recognised as a public right of way. If use has been open and without interference, the law assumes that the owner had intended to dedicate it as a right of way. Paths may be claimed either by user evidence, historical evidence or a combination of both.

In the 1970s and 80s, RA members opened up many footpaths and bridleways in Berkshire that local people had forgotten existed.

Old maps show this route in Hampshire as an important link in the highway network but if it is not claimed by 2026, the opportunity to use it will be lost.

As a result of the CRoW Act, councils now also have a duty to prepare Rights of Way **Improvement Plans**. The idea behind this new concept is for Local Access Forums (made up of users and those who own or manage the countryside) to make recommendations that will influence government officers and elected members in carrying out their duties, for example, by advising on policies and strategies, etc. A good opportunity for walkers to raise the profile of rights of way.

One of the Highway Authority's established tasks is to receive complaints regarding any path problems and to request the owner to take the appropriate action, or failing that, to carry out the work themselves and to charge the landowner. Rights of Way Officers will often be unaware of a problem until it is reported to them. Unless you know otherwise, address a path **problem report** to the county council (or unitary authority) as they are the legitimate Highway Authority, even though a few non-unitary district councils carry out this function on their behalf.

Rights of Way Officers work under a range of different

departmental headings such as Highways, Environment, Leisure, Countryside, depending on the authority. Any correspondence you mark for their attention should get forwarded to the appropriate department.

You can use a path report form available for the purpose, or simply 'do your own thing'. Tell them what the problem is and mark the position clearly on a copy of the map. Keep a copy for reference. Officers will refer to the definitive map to find the parish and path number, then log this information onto their data base. Don't expect instant results, but remember that many of the paths we use today were difficult or impossible to use 10 or 20 years ago and there is no doubt that the more walkers who report a problem, the further up the list it can go. Dangerous situations will get top priority and should be made safe within 24 hours.

Barbed wire on a stile serves no purpose except to harm unsuspecting users. Report as dangerous.

An important means of **enforcing** the duty of the Highway Authority to prevent obstructions on our rights of way was created by the CRoW Act, 2000. This adds a new section130A to the Highways Act 1980, whereby the public may now serve a notice on the authority, requesting them to secure the removal of an obstruction (if not one of the specified exceptions) and take the case to the magistrate's court if they do not get satisfaction. Providing certain criteria are met, magistrates can make an order requiring the obstruction to be removed.

Remember, the Highway Authority's fundamental duty is to protect the rights of the public and to act against those who seek to interrupt those rights. In future, new **cross-compliance** measures could see grants to farmers withheld if they do not keep their paths in good order. It would be nice to think so.

Chance Encounters
Being prepared for the unexpected

Most of our local countryside is a living, working environment and has been so for hundreds of years. To an extent, that is what makes it more interesting and more of a challenge than a walk in the park. If you think it is full of problems, consider how relatively tame it is compared to a jungle wilderness, full of creepy-crawlies! The following should also help, and remember, the law is on your side.

If you meet an **obstruction**, check with the map to confirm that you are actually on the right of way. This will also help you to report the problem to the Highway Authority when you get home. Anything which blocks the highway should be reported, e.g. crops, trees, a locked gate or rubbish, etc.

In the meantime, if you can remove it (carrying a small pair of secateurs to cut back the brambles can be

It is the responsibility of the owner to remove a fallen tree or overhanging growth from a path wherever it occurs.

useful) or easily get around it so as to be able to continue your walk, then you may do so. If the offending obstruction is a standing crop, you have the right to walk through it. However, walkers who are the first to tread-out a path like this need to be confident about where the right of way goes and should keep in single file. Subsequent walkers will be pleased to find it more evident and less intimidating to use. Trying to follow the field edge instead is trespass – and who knows where you might end up? It can also cause more damage and does nothing to help others find the correct path.

If the path crosses a **garden**, walkers should not feel discouraged. Whatever has been done, it cannot detract from the public's legitimate right to use the path. Good waymarking is useful here. Often the boundary of a property will have been extended at some time, perhaps to include part of an adjoining field, (permission for change-of-use is required), thus effectively incorporating the path within the owner's curtilage. Walkers may like to think of it this way: *it's not our path that goes through the garden – it's actually their garden, that goes across our footpath.*

This golf club set an example ...

Walkers should not feel intimidated if the path crosses a **golf course**, both sides need to be considerate. On the fairway, ramblers should be aware (not 'beware') of golfers. But, equally, we have a right to expect golfers to be considerate towards us. For this to happen, both walkers and golfers need to know precisely where the right of way exists. Waymarks or marker posts can be important in these situations. When a new course or layout is proposed, it is generally more satisfactory for the natural line of a path to be maintained and for the

... that others still need to follow.

Where two passions meet.
A golf-course with the raised
profile of the original footpath
still preserved.

design to take account of it than for it to be diverted, or worse still, ignored.

We would expect golfers, before playing, to familiarise themselves with a plan showing the layout of the course and any rights of way. Signs on the path itself can advise walkers that the route is about to cross a fairway (and the direction of play). However, it is equally important that signs warn players to be cautious as walkers may be crossing and they have right of way.

Barbed wire is a devilish invention. Even its proximity can detract from the pleasure of walking a path. Barbed

Barbed wire on fenced paths
should be held away from walkers
... or a strand of plain wire added
on the near-side for protection.

wire across the path is an illegal obstruction and needs very urgent attention and on a stile, it can be a real danger to unsuspecting users. Where the farmer insists that a fence alongside the path has to be made of barbed wire to stop it from being pushed over by the cattle, for example, it should be held away, or on the outside of the posts with an additional strand of plain wire on the inside to protect walkers. The Highways Act 1980 enables a council to deal with this as a nuisance to users if necessary. Ask yourself if it is possible to pass another walker coming the other way without feeling intimidated, getting injured or tearing your clothing on a windy day.

Report barbed-wire too close to the path as a nuisance and across the path as an obstruction.

Permanent and temporary **electric fences** across the path can also be classed as an obstruction unless adequately insulated or an insulated handle provided so that it may be easily unhooked to enable users to pass safely. A sign must also be displayed so that walkers are not caught unaware.

Walkers can also easily be deterred from using a public right of way by a misleading sign or notice, or by a fierce dog kept close to the path. Any form of

A temporary electric-wire fence, suitably lowered and insulated where it crosses the path.

A sprung-wire electric fence across the path needs the yellow warning sign attached; use the insulated handle to unhook it.

Walkers have a right to use a way without intimidation. Owner advised and sign removed.

The dog 'Dazer'

intimidation or nuisance which makes you feel uncomfortable about your free use of the way is likely to be an offence. Do make an effort to report any of these issues to the Highway Authority, whether or not someone is actually injured, so that action can be taken to benefit users in the future.

There is a small device that some walkers find effective against the unwanted attention of dogs. The ultra high-pitched sound emitted by a small hand-held device called a Dazer is harmless, but it is only effective at quite short range and rather directional, so you cannot point it at two dogs at once, for example. Alternatively, if you are concerned, it is best to stand still, avoid eye contact and turn your body slightly away as a non-threatening gesture.

If your route comes to a field containing cattle, it is wise to stop and assess the situation. Nobody wants to be caught unawares. Often it will be a herd of dairy **cows**. The most common breeds are Friesians and Holsteins; both are black and white. A dairy herd will usually be quite near the farm. Cows as well as bulls can have horns,

Fortunately, Highland cattle, with their distinctive long pointed horns, are usually mild-mannered creatures.

Confidence and curiosity: cattle are often more at ease if the path is frequently used by walkers.

A beef bull with suckler herd.

so look for the udders between their back legs. When cows have calves, the udder with its four teats is larger because it is producing milk. The line under the belly is smooth. **Heifers**, young cows that have not had a calf, are the same but with an undeveloped udder. A beef bull may be present in a field with dairy cows or heifers.

Cows have a very strong maternal instinct to protect their calves and in these circumstances, potentially the more dangerous. They can be particularly aggressive towards dogs and there have been occasional reports of problems with walkers. If they have young calves, walk quietly around them keeping well away. Never walk between the mother and her calf. Don't feel obliged to keep strictly to the line of the path.

A group of heifers is naturally inquisitive. This can seem rather disconcerting, so try to stay calm and proceed with outward authority. If necessary, take a step towards them, shout and wave your arm or your stick, if you've thought to pick one up. Walk, don't run.

Bulls have a smooth, hairless scrotum suspended between the back legs and a tuft of hair underneath the belly. They may have a ring in their nose. It is advisable

A suckler herd will be a mixture of different sizes ...

suckler cows ...

bull calves ...

of various ages, and possibly a beef bull. Keep your distance!

A group of inquisitive young bullocks or heifers will all be the same size. If necessary, stand your ground. (See also photo on title page)

The recommended advisory sign designed not to deter walkers from their right to use the path.

to treat all bulls with extreme caution, especially if their cows are getting upset. **Bullocks** are similar but with much less bone and muscle development and the scrotum is small. Bullocks are normally the quietest of them all, but always need to be watched.

Since 1981, the law has allowed a farmer to keep a beef bull over ten months old in fields through which a right of way passes, provided it is accompanied by cows or heifers. There will only ever be one mature bull with a herd. No bull should ever be on its own in a field with a public footpath. The Health and Safety Executive (HSE) asks farmers to draw the attention of the public by putting up a sign such as 'Bull in Field', which must be removed or covered when the bull is no longer present, but not to erect a deterrent notice such as 'Beware of the Bull'.

To an extent, any advice must be subjective and none is foolproof. However, the majority of incidents involve walkers who have dogs. RA advice is to keep dogs on leads whenever possible, but you should let go of your dog's lead if a cow or a bull starts acting aggressively and take the shortest route to safety.

Bulls of all the seven recognised dairy breeds are

banned under all circumstances from fields containing a public path. The person accountable for any animal that is known to be dangerous can be liable for damages if it injures someone using the public path. If a previous incident concerning livestock is reported to the HSE and the farmer responsible fails to take preventative measures, he could be held culpable.

Sheep will usually move away from humans. If one or more decide to approach, they may be hand-reared lambs looking for food or company, but if they are well-built stocky rams (or 'tups') with their heads down, it is best not to stay and antagonise them.

Not all rams have big, curly horns.

A friendly lamb (probably hand-reared) – but wash your hands before you have that picnic.

Horses are quite tame creatures, so they often get closer than most walkers would like. They can also be unpredictable, so unless you are confident, they are best avoided or ignored. Owners prefer walkers not to feed them as it can cause excitable behaviour and a jealous attack between the horses.

Walkers can be vulnerable at main **road** crossings. If there is a footbridge, it will be drawn on the map. However, our map may not differentiate between a path

The main road is in a cutting with the over-bridge clearly visible on the map. ✓

Here, the footpath and dual-carriageway appear to be on the same level, so this is probably a dangerous grade-crossing. ❗

This bridleway has been realigned, so it almost certainly goes under the road here. ✓

The A34 trunk road is on an embankment here, so the track may pass under it. ❓

UNIVERSITY COLLEGE
THIS BRIDLE WAY IS
OPEN TO THE PUBLIC
IN WINTER 7AM-8·30PM
IN SUMMER 7AM-11PM

Exceptionally, public use of a way can be limited, as here through an Oxford College.

that passes underneath the road and a path that crosses on the tarmac surface (a level or 'grade' crossing). Very close inspection of the map detail can sometimes offer a clue. Otherwise, as the OS admits, 'It will be self-evident at the location'. So, if the road is actually fenced off or too dangerous to cross, you may have to retrace your steps.

Unfortunately, limitations of scale generally preclude the map from telling us beforehand if a metalled road has a footway or pavement alongside it. Where there is not a satisfactory verge, walkers should keep in single file and face the oncoming traffic, except at a bend, where it may be necessary with extreme care to cross over some distance beforehand and keep to the outside of the curve. Wear light coloured outer clothing and in poor visibility, or if it is getting dark and you do not have any reflective gear, draw attention to your presence by holding out a large area of the map by your side into the road.

A sign of good practice. Walkers may choose to wait until particles have settled, or consider an alternative route.

Should you find that the field ahead of you is being sprayed with **pesticides**, it obviously makes sense to consider taking an alternative route if possible – a particularly wise precaution if the spray is actually drifting across the line of the path. No farmer should be attempting to do it on a windy day. Government guidelines state that the path should not be sprayed when nearby crops are being treated. In reality, this is clearly difficult when a path bisects the field. The RA is pressing for new measures, such as requiring farmers to keep records and to make them available to the public via a third party. A temporary notice advising walkers that the field has been treated and to proceed with care is considered reasonable – all the more so if the path has been kept clear in accordance with the law and there is therefore no likelihood of bare arms and legs brushing against the standing crop.

To protect a crop (especially organic produce) from damage, a farmer may set-up a **bird scarer**, a propane gas gun with a photo-electric cell to trigger an

A gas-gun designed to startle birds, not to kill them.

Make sure that you only use the side handle to open this type of double farm gate. Check that there is no alternative pedestrian access first.

This contraption can be referred to in Berkshire by the derogatory term 'Hampshire Gate' (and vica versa). Open by lifting the chain or wire loop off the post and stepping through the collapsed wire fence. Fortunately rare.

explosion. It is important that it is positioned with care so as to avoid the risk of surprising passers-by and never on or next to the path itself. It could be partly hidden by straw bales set up as a baffle to concentrate the sound over the crop and reduce noise levels elsewhere. A small notice pointing out its presence and a note regarding timing can be helpful. Despite their appearance, nothing is actually discharged from the barrel.

Unintentional **trespass** can be the result of losing your way or trying to avoid an obstruction. It is a civil wrong and not a crime, providing you are careful not to damage any property. If you are challenged, an apology will usually defuse the situation, If you thought perhaps an obstruction or misleading waymark was responsible, this could be a good opportunity to draw the landowner's attention to it.

Should you come upon a horse being ridden on a footpath or a vehicle being driven along a bridleway, then an act of trespass is being committed unless they have the landowner's permission or own the land themselves. However, that does not give landowners the right to cause a nuisance or damage the public highway.

October heralds the start of the pheasant **shooting** season. For the next four months, the tranquillity of the English countryside can be interrupted occasionally (except Sundays) by the sound of gun fire. However, any footpaths within range of the guns should have a marshal posted at either end. They will ask walkers to stop for a few moments until it is safe to continue. Over the years, there have been no reported problems with this arrangement, although the sight of birds falling out of the sky may not be everyone's ideal image to take home.

More Walking Opportunities

Local areas with public access

In addition to the linear access afforded to us by the public rights of way network, a number of areas of open, uncultivated countryside are available for the walker to enjoy. The extent of some areas will be highlighted on our OS map, with the site of others only indicated by a symbol. You may also come upon quite a few not marked on the map at all because access is based on a local or temporary agreement.

The latest Explorer maps show **access land** designated under the Countryside and Rights of Way Act 2000. This is wholly or predominately mountain, moor, heath or

Sugglestone Down in west Berkshire; an escarpment of unimproved downland now with open access on foot.

A typical downland escarpment, with public access, but too steep to take advantage of.

downland. Look for the light, yellow tint with pale, orange, boundary ribbon. However, some of this land is classified as excepted land. The list includes race courses, golf courses, quarries, etc. and any land within 20 metres of a house. So, even if it is coloured yellow, walkers are restricted to rights of way here. Also, although land over 600 metres (almost 2,000 feet) automatically qualifies as access land, that is more than twice as high as anything we have in south-east England, with Walbury Hill in Berkshire 297m and Leith Hill in Surrey just 294m.

New access land is relatively sparse in the south-east region, except for isolated patches of heathland and some unimproved chalk grassland on the escarpments of the Downs. In practice, some of these areas, which may never have been ploughed, can also be almost too steep to walk on and, where areas are bounded by fences and hedgerows, legitimate access may only be possible from

1   From the car park, access land along the escarpment could be used to link existing rights of way.

2   If there are no stiles or gates, our way could be restricted by these fences.

3   Open access to the west is currently limited after a kilometre.

4   Registered Common Land. No need to keep strictly to the bridleway alongside the properties.

5   The rough grassland shown is more likely to offer interesting wildlife than a direct path-line across this common.

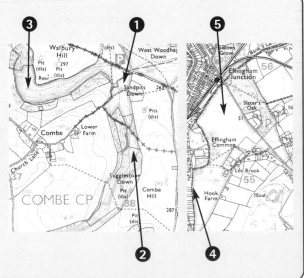

existing rights of way. In due course, specific access points will be agreed and this information added to the map.

Walkers also need to bear in mind that landowners are able to restrict access for up to 28 days a year on the grounds of conservation, heritage and land management (except public holidays and most weekends). Requests for longer-term restrictions have to be considered by the Local Access Forum. Look out for local signs, or check the Countryside Agency website beforehand. See page 102 for details. Besides the necessity for a dog to be under control where there is livestock, walkers should also note the specific requirement in the Act for them to be kept on leads during the period 1st March to end of July.

Part of Effingham Common in Surrey. (See map extract, item 5)

Similarly portrayed in yellow for the first time on the new maps are the areas of registered **common land**, with any areas that are wooded showing up as a yellowish-green tint. These are scattered across the region and range in size from the 1,350-acre (550 hectares) Greenham and Crookham Commons to a number of much smaller areas that include village ponds and even strips of roadside verge. The public has the same qualified statutory right of access to them all on foot.

Commons are a legacy from a time when much of our land was wild and used *in common* by the local population. Most of the large areas of rural common land are now owned by local authorities and managed solely for public enjoyment, but three-quarters of the land to which these rights still apply is in private hands.

A special feature of many commons is that they remain largely unfenced. Unfortunately, Councils have the power, but not the duty, to take court action against those who encroach upon them or erect unlawful fencing

The National Trust owns more country and coastline than any other conservation body.

Bourne Wood. Part of the Forestry Commission's extensive Alice Holt Forest open to walkers.

Welcome!

By agreement with the owner you are welcome to walk here.

A new woodland is being created for your enjoyment and that of future generations, with the help of the Forestry Commission.

Forestry Commission

Temporary woodland access – not on the map.

without obtaining the Secretary of State's consent. A recent survey by the Open Spaces Society indicates that many commons have been desecrated and our right to fresh air and exercise may often be seriously restricted.

The depiction of any land that is permanently open and held by the **National Trust**, the **Woodland Trust** and the **Forestry Commission** is also now highlighted on our map as a bright green wooded area. In each case, the landowner concerned is no longer identified on the map, although the larger coniferous plantations are usually owned by the Forestry Commission.

Paths and nature trails waymarked on the ground generally follow the established paths and tracks shown in black on our map. These can often enable us to avoid roads and to join up rights of way in the wider countryside. Be prepared to accept some temporary restrictions where trees are being felled, for example.

Largely as a result of pressure from the RA, the Forestry Commission propose to make dedication agreements on all its freehold land in England by the end of 2006. That will secure a right for future generations to walk there, even if land is sold on. They also issue licences for various activities such as horse-riding and husky dog-racing, etc. through the woods – so you could be in for a surprise.

Walkers may also come upon woodland open to us as part of a local agreement, whereby the Forestry Commission manages the land on behalf of a private owner. Look for the 'Welcome' signs. Unfortunately, due to the temporary nature of such arrangements, these areas cannot be identified on our map.

The best place for specimen trees; large areas of Windsor Great Park (above) and Swinley Forest (left) are owned by the Crown Estate and open to the public.

Considerable land in Berkshire is owned by the Crown and open to the public for walking. **Windsor Great Park** is the most obvious example and a useful large-scale map showing these areas is published by our Ramblers' Association Group from information supplied by the estate office. (Copies are available locally or by post from us. See page 102 for contact details.)

In addition, 2,600 acres of land at **Swinley Forest**, just south of Bracknell, is managed by the Borough Council on behalf of the Crown Estate. Although the tracks shown on our Explorer map do correspond reasonably well with the routes available to walkers here, a map showing the trails and limit of public access is on sale from *The Look Out Information Centre.* This can avoid the possibility of getting lost in a situation where one track through the pine forest, looks very much like any other.

For clues to other areas of countryside with public access on foot, look for the **Nature Reserve** annotation and the bird symbol shown in blue on the map. Information regarding the extent of the site and the paths that we can use is usually displayed on site.

Nature reserves; look out for the blue bird-symbol on the map.

One of the most celebrated large areas of woodland to be identified by this blue symbol is **Burnham Beeches** in south Buckinghamshire. Here, 600 acres were bought by the City of London Corporation in 1880 and since then the area has been maintained as a nature reserve with free public access. Details of other privately owned woodlands that are not identified on the map but where visitors are welcome, (such as those on the Englefield Estate in north Hampshire), may be found in 'Exploring Woodlands', a series of booklets prepared by the Woodland Trust, published by Collins.

Country parks can be a good introduction to walking in the fresh air and are ideal for the elderly and less able, with plenty of clear, well-defined footpaths. They are annotated on the map in black with a blue tourist symbol, but again the extent is not currently shown and we may find ourselves struggling to rely on the fine detail of our map or referring to plans displayed on site. Most are owned by the local authority, but a few, such as Wellington Country Park, are a commercial operation and although some additional facilities and attractions are available here, people must pay for access to countryside that is freely available elsewhere to everyone – if they know where to look.

Country parks; easy, convenient and ideal for those with limited mobility – otherwise few surprises, except perhaps the occasional dog scuffle.

The **Blackwater Valley**, on the borders of Berkshire, Hampshire and Surrey, is an attractive public open space of considerable length. It is easily accessible by rail. A partnership between the local authorities has transformed this area over the past 20 years. Former gravel extraction sites are now established wildlife areas and there is a network of surfaced river and lakeside paths suitable for everyone. Unfortunately, none of these have yet been dedicated as public rights of way. Only the 23-mile-long recreational route is highlighted on the map.

Part of Blackwater Valley.

Few people realise how much **Ministry of Defence** land is potentially available to the public whenever this is compatible with its primary military purpose. Local communities make good use of the large training areas either side of the Blackwater Valley, for example. Much of this often wild and rugged heathland is usually open but cannot be highlighted on the map because it is classified as excepted land. Dry training exercise areas, where live ammunition is not used, are shown by a series

These RA members have just followed a definitive bridleway across rugged heathland owned by the MOD at Bagshot.

Squaddies on a ramble ... at the double!

of open, red arrow heads. Walkers should keep to the established tracks and not touch any metal objects on the ground. There are also some public rights of way across these areas which are not affected.

The most restricted areas, for example, near the military establishments at Sandhurst, Purbright and Aldershot, are clearly identified on the map by the words 'Danger Area' with solid, red arrow heads along the fence line. These areas are often closed to the public, especially during the week, so that live firing can take place on the ranges. Do not enter if the red flags are flying. Details of the sites around the country that are actively promoted, are listed in a booklet available from the Defence Estates. See page 102 for contact details.

National Parks and **Areas of Outstanding Natural Beauty** (AONBs) are considered to include some of our finest landscapes. However, these designations do not give the public any additional general right of public access. The land remains largely in private ownership and the designation is primarily intended to conserve the area and protect it from inappropriate development. On the latest OS Explorer maps, National Park boundaries are shown using a ribbon of light magenta dashes. The extent of an AONB (for example the North Wessex Downs, Surrey Hills or the Chilterns) is only indicated on the back cover of the relevant map. Some larger-scale road atlases show the area in more detail.

Conservation Walks are access opportunities created under the government-funded Countryside Stewardship and Environmentally Sensitive Areas schemes, both of which are designed to protect wildlife and improve the landscape. Because each site is open to us nationally for only a limited period of up to 10 years, these often little-known areas are not shown on commercial mapping. A plan will be displayed when you come upon a site, or details can be obtained from the Department of Environment, Food and Rural Affairs (Defra). See page 102 for contact details. Changes to these schemes are likely in the future, but funding to encourage farmers to make their land more walker-friendly looks set to continue.

Access to Countryside Stewardship land is only for a limited period.

We hope that local authorities and some landowners can in future be persuaded to dedicate parks, gardens, recreational areas and other land that they own as **public open space** by using section 16 of the CRoW Act 2000. The extent of it would then be clearly visible on OS maps. Everyone in the urban fringe, for example, would also be able to identify the most direct and attractive route either to the wider countryside or for a walk into town.

Walkers Welcomed
How to leave a good impression

We hope that you now feel inspired with sufficient knowledge and understanding to explore your local countryside and enjoy it with confidence. The following hints should ensure there is a welcome waiting for you when you get there.

Of course walkers need to behave responsibly, otherwise landowners will be justifiably upset, but there are a few aspects of the country scene which are simply not part of everyday urban life. A field of long grass, for example, is actually a crop grown for grazing or to make hay or silage. The farmer is not required to keep a route through grass clear, so if it has not already been trodden-out, we should keep as close to the line of the path as possible to avoid flattening the grass elsewhere, as this will make it difficult to cut and harvest.

Where there is grass in the field, stay on the path to avoid trampling elsewhere, so that it can be cut for hay.

If a path has not yet been reinstated, walking in single file will help to establish the line for others.

Walkers can take a dog into the countryside as a 'natural accompaniment' and usually an enthusiastic companion, but they must not be allowed to run through standing crops or disturb wildlife. Dogs should never be off the lead where there is livestock. On designated access land, there is new requirement for dogs to be on a short lead for the whole five-month period from March to July.

Dog owners also have a duty to ensure that their pet does not threaten or harm other members of the public. Owners also need to be vigilant using bridleways, where dogs may upset horses, and on byways, where they will be at risk from vehicles.

At rail crossings, wait behind the stile until it is safe to cross.

At unguarded rail crossings it is essential that users observe the warning signs and wait behind the stile or gate if there is any sight or sound of an approaching train. This is not only for their own safety; reports from drivers concerned by walkers waiting beside the track, only adds to pressure for these paths to be closed altogether.

To avoid adding to congestion on country roads and

Support rural services. Enjoy the view and the possibility of a linear walk.

You can't always be sure of finding an old vacuum cleaner on the public footpath!

worrying about security whenever a car is left in an isolated spot, consider using local puplic transport if the opportunity exists. Considerable subsidies have gone into supporting rural bus services recently and currently, GroupSave promotions enable four adults to travel for the price of two with some rail companies on weekend and off-peak services. It's ideal for linear walks. Try it sometime, especially on longer day-trips; nobody should spend more time behind the wheel than walking in the country.

Although not entirely blameless themselves, farmers do get pretty irate about litter discarded by ramblers, they assume, but more likely thrown from passing vehicles or by those who have managed to stagger a few paces from the local pub. We can obviously set a good example, but if you should come upon someone discarding litter or rubbish on the footpath you might ask them, *Don't you want that?* Their reply is always, no, they do not. The response, *Well we don't want it either,* neatly by-passes any discussion about it being only garden refuse or compost that will rot down. Whatever it is, if they don't want it, then neither do we – thank you very much.

Although there is no regular highway cleaning in the countryside, the public amenities or technical services department at the Unitary or District Council are responsible for clearing rubbish and litter, providing it is on the right of way. They often rely on the public to identify these sites, especially when they are not visible from the road.

We suggest it is best to leave all gates as you find them – and as we have always said, leave all wild flowers for others to enjoy.

Some Popular Misconceptions

- **A stile indicates the existence of a public footpath.**
  Stiles are sometimes erected, other than on public paths, solely for a landowner's personal convenience.

- **If a path is not walked for a certain number of years, then it will cease to exist.**
  A public path will only cease to exist after it has been *officially* extinguished.

- **If a path is not visible on the ground, then it does not exist.**
  What *does* exist is a public right. There does not have to be any physical presence.

- **If someone encroaches onto the public highway, they can, after a number of years, lay claim to the land for themselves.**
  They may be able to stake a claim to some land, but *not* if it is part of a highway.

- **Most roads also have a footpath alongside.**
  Strictly speaking, and to avoid any confusion, a roadside path should be referred to as a footway or a pavement.

A stile, erected just to access a small plantation of young trees.

Not the type of path for which any Rights of Way Department would be responsible.

Prohibited ...

end of a restriction.

- **When an advertisement appears or a notice is posted stating that a Highway Authority has 'Made an Order' to divert or extinguish a path, it is too late to object.**
  No, an Order only comes into effect <u>if</u> it is subsequently *confirmed*.

- **Rights of way are automatically lost after years of obstruction or neglect.**
  Not true, but a Highway Authority might consider that a path was not needed for public use if problems that had existed for years had never been reported.

- **A sign showing a mode of transport within a red circle tells us that the way can be used by that method.**
  Wrong. The form of transport shown is banned. When struck through with a red bar, it actually indicates the limit or extent of that ban.

- **The path crosses my land, so I can close it if I want to.**
  Virtually all rights of way cross private land, but a farmer or landowner cannot close a path by taking unilateral action.

- **All ramblers must wear bobble hats.**
  Only if all farmers insist on tying up their trousers with a piece of string!

Kids in the Country

Some tips on how children can have an enjoyable day out – with a little help and encouragement from their parents

- Ask your children if they would like to go for a hike or a picnic, explore the woods, or head for the hills. A walk can sound dull and uneventful.
- Do let them take some friends so they can share the experience. Put a copy of 'I-Spy in the Country' in their pocket.
- It is better to make an outing too short than too long.
- Ask them to help you find the way by looking out for the next feature shown on the map or in the guidebook – or try 'hunt the next waymark'.
- If they are old enough to read and know 'left' from 'right', give them a guidebook to use. There is stimulation and satisfaction in finding the way.
- Try to find an area that has lots of short paths. Avoid straight and boring tracks where you can see the way ahead for miles. Remember, paths look even longer when you are not very tall!

- Consider having an aim such as picking blackberries, or an objective such as a viewpoint or a lake; water in any form always holds a fascination.
- Take the time to enjoy any unplanned 'distractions' that you come across.
- Don't worry if they get into a bit of a mess when they kick leaves or slip in the mud.
- Have some refreshments with you and get ice creams all round if you are lucky enough to find a village shop open. Most pubs now welcome children.

- Remember to take some spare clothing, If there is a sudden heavy shower, consider finding somewhere snug to shelter. (It is likely to be the experience they tell everyone about afterwards.)
- In the woods, they may be able to play or hide, but remember not to disturb the wildlife and to leave wild flowers for others to enjoy.
- Linear walks using a bus or train take more planning but can be especially rewarding, with more varied scenery and a greater sense of achievement.
- Appear to be more tired and exhausted than *they* are!
- When you find a nice spot, take a well earned rest.

At the end of the day they will be more confident ... you will have got to know them better!

The Great Crop Mystery
Name some and see how they grow

Visitors to the countryside are often presented with the opportunity to read about the history and even the geology of an area they are visiting from a guide book or a leaflet, but the type and nature of a crop that might surround them on all sides is often a mystery. The appearance of arable (from *aro* – to plough) fields can change quite dramatically from one year to the next as farmers change or rotate their crops. We hope that these few notes will enable walkers to identify those most likely to be encountered in this area of south-east England together with some of the more unusual.

The three main cereal crops: wheat, barley and oats.

Wheat, Oats, and Barley: These staple crops, commonly referred to collectively as corn or cereals, are usually drilled (i.e. sown in rows) during the autumn to provide, for example, winter wheat. Some farmers choose to plant cereals during the spring, leaving weedy stubble over the winter months to benefit farmland birds and insects, or for other uses. Combine harvesting begins in mid July and goes on for several weeks.

The majority of the grain is stored in towers known as silos and much of the dried stalks (straw) is baled for use as bedding for livestock. Almost half the wheat crop (feed wheat) and a third of the oats will go into quality animal feed. The top grade wheat is milled into flour for bread and high quality barley is used to make malt for the brewing of beer and lager. A proportion of the oats ends up as porridge and in muesli and multi-grain bread.
Grass: In the first few weeks, newly sown grass has a

Wild poppies; ready to germinate when sprays are not used.

The white Lupin; another legume becoming more widely grown as a source of protein for animals.

very similar appearance to corn, although the blades appear thinner or finer than cereals. There is no requirement for a farmer to avoid planting grass on a path. It may either be grazed or cut for hay from late June onwards when it is knee high and the seed-heads have formed. When thoroughly dry, it will be gathered up into rectangular or large, round bales.

Grass that is to be preserved as silage will be cut by mowing in May, with generally two more cuts during the summer. The grass is pressed down in a silage clamp and covered to exclude the air so that it can ferment. Some farmers now prefer to make silage in individual bales wrapped in plastic and to sow a grass and clover mixture.

Maize; insignificant in May, (top right) almost impenetrable by September (above). Do not leave the path or you may get lost!

Maize: Young maize plants start to appear in early May and in the spring it is difficult to imagine that they will grow to over six feet in the next five months. Cross-field paths therefore need to be established *more* than one metre wide if the route is to remain usable later in the season. Although the seed-head is often recognised as corn on the cob or sweet-corn, it is usually grown in this part of the country as food for cattle, with the whole plant being mechanically harvested in September or October and made into silage.

Linseed; fine, delicate and rarely any problem for walkers.

After harvesting the linseed, the waste straw is allowed to be burnt (under license) as it is very tough and blocks subsequent cultivation machinery.

Not just a pretty face; strips of short-stemmed sunflowers are grown for wild and game-bird seed.

Linseed: This is the crop that can turn the fields a pale blue colour in early summer. The slender, foot-high plants have delicate little flowers and, after harvesting in September, most of the linseed will be used in the manufacture of high-grade oil for paints, varnishes and linoleum. Flax is the longer-stemmed variety which contains fibres that are extracted for linen production.

Dark fields of oil-seed rape in winter become recognisable and blindingly bright by early summer.

Oilseed Rape: The bright, yellow patches that appear in the countryside during the spring are caused by the flowers of this crop which everyone thought was mustard when it first appeared in the 1970s. In fact, it is a member of the brassica family which does include mustards. It is usually sown in late August and walkers often assume that the young cabbage-like plants that become established in the fields during October and November (look for the crinkled outline of the long leaves) are unlikely to cause a problem.

In fact, once the growing season starts again towards the end of February, a cross-field path will soon become difficult and then impossible to use unless a clear width of least 2.5 metres is established at the outset. This is because soon after the crop has flowered and the seed set in June, the shoulder-high plants will start to collapse, making the path absolutely impenetrable until combine harvested in late July. Rape is a multi-purpose crop, grown to produce vegetable oils for both human consumption and industrial use – everything from cooking oil to biodiesel fuel.

Field Peas & Beans: These legumes are sown either in autumn or spring and harvested from July to September as a nutritious feed for livestock, particularly cattle. They also make up a small part of the diet of pigs and poultry.

Root Crops: Apart from a few potatoes, most root crops in this part of the country are grown to feed livestock. Turnips, swedes, mangolds and fodder beet are rich in energy and are highly digestible for sheep, cattle and pigs. Any beet grown to produce sugar for human consumption is concentrated near the processing factories further to the east.

Broad beans are starting to make this path too narrow.

Stubble turnips being grazed by sheep. (left)

Unlike white clover, the red variety shown here can grow to knee height before cutting. (right)

Hemp; a versatile non-food crop that grows so fast that pests and disease don't stand a chance.

Fibre Hemp: This eight-foot-high, cane-like plant is very occasionally grown, not for the hallucinatory effects for which as a drug it is well known (this variety is very low in cannabinoids), but for the fibres that it produces. They are used in the production of board, bank notes and more.

The only question still to be answered is who makes corn circles and why? Perhaps it is best that that remains a mystery.

Working for Walkers
Advice, action and influence

Inevitably, you will come upon situations not covered by this booklet – highway law is a complicated subject. Rights of way have been under-funded for many years and, despite their obligations, Highway Authorities still often fail to give countryside access the priority it deserves.

Almost every day the **Ramblers' Association** (RA) and the **Open Spaces Society** (OSS) receive news of countryside under threat from developers, blocked or dangerous footpaths and lawbreakers who bar the public from rights of way. Without constant vigilance Britain's countryside and the paths and open spaces that enable us to enjoy it could so easily disappear.

Both of these charitable organisations are an important source of authoritative advice on footpath matters. The OSS was founded in 1865 and is Britain's oldest national conservation body. It campaigns to protect common land, village greens, open spaces and public paths, and the people's right to enjoy them.

The RA can draw on years of experience as Britain's largest walking organisation to advise on footpath law and how best to deal with a problem on the ground. An information service is operated in fulfilment of the RA's charitable aim to encourage walking and is consequently not just available to members but also to the public. The Association also offers a range of publications on all aspects of walking and can provide regional guides to anywhere in England, Scotland or Wales.

Part of the busy Open Spaces Society offices in Henley.

'The countryside speaks to us in the way that nothing else can. It lifts the soul. We will help to educate and inspire people to make full use of their rights in a responsible way.'

Nick Barrett
Ramblers' Association
Chief Executive, 2005

FOOTNOTE: *A booklet of this size can only give general guidance and information. It is not a definitive statement of the law. However, it should help anyone who previously did not feel confident enough to explore the great outdoors on their own. Those who would like to be fully acquainted with the law should obtain a copy of* Rights of Way; A guide to law and practice *by John Riddall and John Trevelyan, published by the Open Spaces Society and Ramblers' Association.*

The Rambler's Yearbook is a comprehensive accommodation guide, with maps and a compact source of useful information for walkers. It includes local authority addresses and web sites, public transport information, recommended pubs and tea-rooms, plus contact details of Ramblers' areas and groups, associated bodies and organisations. It also contains an equipment directory, a section listing regional guidebooks and long-distance paths cross referenced to the B&B section. Published annually, it is free to members or can be bought from all good bookshops.

Useful addresses

Berkshire Area For details of the individual RA groups in Berkshire contact John Moules, 50 Qualitas, Roman Hill, Bracknell, Berkshire RG12 7QG

Countryside Agency For information about the extent and nature of any restrictions relating to access land. **www.countrysideaccess.gov.uk**

Defence Estates For information about access to MoD land. **tel** 0121 311 2140 • **www.defence-estates.mod.uk**

Defra (Dept. for Environment, Food & Rural Affairs) **www.defra.gov.uk** For details of public access provided under environmental schemes. **http://countrywalks.defra.gov.uk**

East Berks RA Group Publications For price list/order form, send a SAE to PO Box 1357, Maidenhead SL6 7FP **www.eastberksramblers.org**

Open Spaces Society 25A Bell Street, Henley-on-Thames, Oxon RG9 2BA **tel** 01491 573535 • email: hq@oss.org.uk • **www.oss.org.uk**

Ramblers Association Camelford House, 87-90 Albert Embankment, London SE1 7TW **tel** 020 7339 8500 • email: ramblers@london.ramblers.org.uk **www.ramblers.org.uk**

Index

Although **Dave Ramm** has lived most of his adult life near Reading, it was as a child, often running on ahead with the guidebook that he – with his parents, would explore the Surrey hills at week-ends – days that sparked a love of the English countryside.

Later, whilst walking with his own young children he met Peter Nevell, who introduced him to the important work of the Ramblers' Association. From that moment his involvement in countryside access steadily grew; first, by working to clear and open footpaths that had often been neglected for many years, then by leading walks and campaigning to save paths under threat. He is now a local correspondent for the Open Spaces Society.

When he left school Dave started as a cartographer with the Colonial Surveys, mapping far away places from aerial photography. He has always been a rather compulsive cartographer and later on would typically spend the day mapping Milton Keynes and then in the evening draw maps for the Group's Rambling for Pleasure series of guide books.

It was while selling these seven previous titles and talking to other walkers that he realised how often they would ask the same questions: who is responsible for a broken stile, what does this coloured arrow mean, how can we find out where to walk when we are on holiday, and so on. What was needed was a book that presented all the facets of this intriguing subject in a clear and easily assimilated form. This is the result.

'The everlasting lure of round-the-corner, how fascinating it is!'

Christopher Morley,
US author and journalist.
(1890–1957)

Acknowledgements

The author would like to thank the following for their help and advice in preparing this booklet: Elaine Cox, Senior Rights of Way Officer at West Berkshire District Council, Janet Davis, Head of Footpaths Policy at the Ramblers' Association, Colin Dibb for his farming expertise and staff at the Ordnance Survey Customer Services Centre.

Thanks are also due to other members of the East Berkshire R A Group – especially Margaret Bowdery, whose forty years of work for local rights of way has been an inspiration.

The Ramblers' Association is unable to accept liability for any misinterpretation of the law or any other error or omission in the advice in this Group publication.